ROXY'S
LITTLE
BLACK
BLACK
BOOK
OF TIPS &
TRICKS

ROXY'S LITTLE BLACK BOOK OF TIPS & TRICKS

The no-bullsh*t guide to all things PR,
social media, business and
building your brand

ROXY JACENKO

ALLEN&UNWIN
SYDNEY · MELBOURNE · AUCKLAND · LONDON

First published in 2018

Copyright © Roxy Jacenko 2018

Allen & Unwin
83 Alexander Street
Crows Nest NSW 2065
Australia
Phone: (61 2) 8425 0100
Email: info@allenandunwin.com
Web: www.allenandunwin.com

A catalogue record for this book is available from the National Library of Australia

ISBN 978 1 76052 911 6

Internal design by Alissa Dinallo
Set in 9/15 pt Gotham by Midland Typesetters, Australia
Printed and bound in Australia by McPherson's Printing Group

10 9 8 7 6 5

The paper in this book is FSC® certified. FSC® promotes environmentally responsible, socially beneficial and economically viable management of the world's forests.

CONTENTS

INTRODUCTION

Why a business book?

The fact that I'm sitting here writing a business book when, at school, I was the student who read the crib notes rather than the actual books is rather ironic. However, if I've proved anything over the years, it's that you needn't be the smartest girl in the room or get the highest marks (heck, I didn't even go to uni!) to succeed in PR or business. If I can do it, anyone can. The trick is to be willing to give up your excuses and consistently put in the work.

As the founder and director of four companies,

Sweaty Betty PR, The Ministry of Talent, Social Union and Pixie's Bows, I've learnt a lot about what to do AND what not to do in business. My specialisation is PR, generating buzz and publicity for my clients. However, over the years I've learnt to adapt, grow and take on challenges and opportunities I could never have even dreamt of when I first started out.

In fact, I guarantee that if you travelled back in time and told 24-year-old Roxy that by 2018 she would have started three more companies, got married (and had her marriage survive a year while her husband was in jail), had two children, penned three novels and a non-fiction book, starred on *Celebrity Apprentice*, survived breast cancer, hosted more than five sell-out 'In Conversation with Roxy Jacenko' seminars and become a brand ambassador for some truly fabulous products, she would spit out her skim mocha (my coffee of choice back then) in fits of laughter.

So how did it all happen?

Everything I've done when it comes to business has been guided by my intuition, common sense and an unbreakable work ethic, as well as a whole lot of blood, sweat and tears. In a sense, you could say I've worked to my own ethos, which has always been 'don't think, do'.

I didn't set out to become a PR or business guru and I certainly didn't set out to become a 'celebrity', 'influencer' or, my personal favourite, 'socialite'. I simply set my mind to doing the best job possible, every single day, building a business and ensuring that I exceeded my clients' expectations.

Of all the titles I've been given in the media over the years, 'socialite' is the one that makes me roll my eyes more than any other. Is it really all that social to be replying to emails at nine on a Saturday night? Is working the door at a client's event after running around all day, packing gift bags, unloading cases of mineral water, chasing caterers, getting ready in five minutes flat and then marking names off a guest list considered socialising? While it may look terribly glamorous from the outside, I can assure you that socialising was off my radar for a long, long time.

When I started Sweaty Betty PR, I didn't know anything other than work. I literally slept at the office! I had no real plan other than to make sh*t happen, ensure clients were ecstatic and just keep putting one foot in front of the other.

If I had made a concrete five- or ten-year plan, would I have planned to create the four companies I have now? Absolutely not! And would it have all worked out the way it has if I had stuck to my beautifully colour-coded implementation plan? I strongly doubt it.

Similarly, if I had just decided one day that I wanted to become an Instagram 'influencer', you can bet your 18-carat-gold tennis bracelet that it wouldn't have worked. Why? Because you can't fake hard work, you can't fake authenticity and, as every successful entrepreneur, or influencer for that matter, will tell you, there is no such thing as overnight success.

Everything I share in my 'In Conversation with Roxy Jacenko' seminars is my personal experience and opinion. I don't sugar-coat it or try to make anything sound more fancy or complex than it needs to be. The insights I share are my truth. These are the actual methods and procedures that work for me and my team. They are authentic, honest and, as anyone who has been in the audience will agree, about as real as you can get (curse words included—sorry, Mum!).

Together with my team, I've hosted sell-out 'In Conversation with Roxy Jacenko' seminars in Sydney, Melbourne, Perth and the Gold Coast, with more on the way. Through developing the seminar concept, along with answering audience questions, it's become evident that a complete guide featuring all my tips and tricks would make a handy reference for publicists, students and anyone interested in growing their own business.

My first three books, *Strictly Confidential*, *The Rumour Mill* and *In the Spotlight*, gave a glimpse into the world of PR. While they were fictional, they were inspired by my real-life experiences and gave a pretty fair account of the whirlwind craziness that is running a PR firm. Entertaining, yes! However, you would probably class them as juicy, guilty-pleasure reads more than resourceful and practical guides to PR, social media, branding and business.

So, with that in mind, I decided to create a no-nonsense, easy-to-digest round-up of all my tips and tricks.

This book is for you!

I've written this book for aspiring publicists, those who already work in the industry, anyone who wants to grow their existing business or anyone dreaming of starting their own business.

I've broken down the content into five distinct chapters: Career, Business, PR, Social Media and Life. Within the chapters you will find short-and-sweet subsections covering everything from emails to events and everything in between.

Each chapter stands alone, so you can refer to them at any time you want a fresh burst of inspiration. However, I strongly suggest reading the whole book in order first so that you have all the background knowledge as each chapter flows to the next. And even if you're about to launch your own small business, for example, I'm sure you'll still find some useful information in the Career chapter.

As with everything I do, I've written this book with candour and honesty. Ask any of my friends and family and they will tell you that, with me, what you see is always what you get! I'm black and white, upfront and an open book. I actually have no filter and always give my honest opinion. Some people love this; others hate it. My honesty has gotten me in trouble over the years—that's for sure—but I'm confident I wouldn't be the businesswoman I am today without it.

I have no doubt that if you have this book in your hands, you're inclined to be the same way. You want an all-access guide to the tips and tricks that have helped me succeed. I've done my very best to compile everything I've spoken about in my seminars and more, with real-life examples to guide and inspire you.

This book is my opportunity to give back to everyone who has supported me over the years. Whether you're the smiling faces in the crowd at my seminar (or, in many cases, seminars—I LOVE seeing people come back a second or even third time!), the ones sending me beautiful emails sharing your success stories or the ones messaging me on Instagram or standing up for me in the comment threads (which can get very interesting at times!), your kindness and support do not go unnoticed. I can sense your passion, commitment and drive to strive for excellence in your careers and businesses and I'm personally inspired after meeting and hearing from so many of you. From the 60-year-old grandmother who is following her passion to create the small business she's always dreamt of, to the 16-year-old high school student who is proactive in making his or her career ambitions a reality, each and every one of you is the reason I hold my seminars and have now written this book.

I hope you enjoy, because this book is for you!

Love,
Roxy xx

CHAPTER 1

CAREER

Study

If I had a dollar for every email I've ever been sent asking me what, when, where and whether to study at university, I'd own another Hermès Birkin bag! It's fair to say it is one of the most common questions I'm asked by school students and aspiring publicists.

It's widely known that I did not go to university. I got part way through a TAFE fashion course before deciding it was not for me. Yes, I was the crazy girl with just four months' experience in PR who opened her own agency without so much as a pass mark in PR 101. More on that later.

When it comes to study and a career in PR, I believe a degree is your base point. It's the bare minimum standard these days to get your foot in the door for work experience and the foundational knowledge you need to build a career. If you don't have a degree or are not at least in the process of getting one, you'd be hard-pressed to even get a look-in when it comes to work experience, let alone an actual job.

Whether you decide to study communications, marketing, business or similar, having a degree demonstrates your ability to commit to something and see it through. It shows that you have drive, dedication and the ability to focus and get a job done.

Studying PR or related courses at university also gives you the technical skills, such as the ability to write well, that are essential in PR. It also gives you an understanding of various strategies, market segments and the media landscape, all key when it comes to performing as a publicist.

However, while I believe that formal qualifications are important, I honestly don't think that having a degree will equip you for life in the job. There are just so many facets of the day-to-day role of a publicist that need to be experienced, so many tasks that can only be taught in a hands-on fashion over an extended period of time and so many 'trade secrets' that you learn on the job. But that aside, when it comes to study, I think it's best to do as I say and not as I did. Sorry!

The PR landscape has changed dramatically since I started out and is now more competitive than ever. While I don't have a hard-and-fast rule about my staff having a university degree (most do, but some do not), there are lots of PR agencies and companies that will expect you to have one.

Yes, I know, three or four years may seem like a long time and you're just dying to work in PR. But I guarantee it will pass by swiftly, especially if you also do work experience while you study. Before you know it, you'll have that all-important degree with your name on it and a sense of accomplishment for having seen it through.

Work experience and internships

This is where the magic happens!

Whether you call it work experience or a formal internship, on-the-job experience is invaluable. I can't emphasise this point enough. While you're at uni, make sure you're getting as much real-world experience as you can. After all, most students have several days a week spare.

Rather than sit around in a café complaining about how many essays you have to write, make the most of your class-free time by seeking a part-time job or internship in your chosen industry.

Regardless of what and where you study, it's only when you have a job that your academic achievements all come together. The practical skills, real-world situations, pressure, expectations and competing demands can't be replicated in a classroom setting. No matter how proficient your press release writing skills or how fantastic your launch strategy, if you don't know the basics—how to deal with clients, how to email the media, how to execute an event for 100 people—then your high distinction average will mean very little.

When looking to employ a new staff member, I value on-the-job experience over and above a university degree. I won't even consider a candidate unless I can see that they've had extensive work experience. Not only does it show me that they have some idea of what's expected in the workplace, but it also demonstrates their initiative and drive.

Importantly, they need to have had more than two weeks of work experience in each workplace! What on earth can you learn in two weeks? I would suggest that three months is the bare minimum needed in order to learn some valuable lessons. Any less, and it's a waste of your time.

Love or loathe the idea, internships are key to getting your start in the industry, especially in PR but also for any jobs in fashion, beauty, marketing or business—you name it. You can never learn too much or have too much experience.

How to make your application stand out for all the right reasons

Over the years I've received hundreds—make that thousands—of emails and letters from work experience hopefuls and job applicants. From elaborate video applications to poorly written three-line resumes, I've seen it all.

While I don't pretend to be an HR guru, trust me, I've had my fair share of interesting staff over the years, and I've become pretty savvy at sorting the genuine ones from the imitations and fakes. Much like fake designer handbags, just don't go there!

Here are some basic elements you must include if you want your application to get a look-in and stand out among a sea of 'fashion- and beauty-loving big fan, would loooooove to work with you' hopefuls. While it may seem glaringly obvious, I can't even tell you how many people get the basics wrong. Or just skip them entirely!

Write a cover letter. That may seem fairly standard, but many an application has dropped into my inbox without one. Clearly explain why you are looking for work experience or why you want the job. Go on to briefly explain your studies and experience and how these are applicable to the role you're applying for. Be honest, to the point and make sure you triple-check for spelling and grammar mistakes. First impressions are priceless!

While I'm on the topic of obvious, be sure to attach your resume. It frustrates me no end when someone emails enquiring about work experience or a job and they don't send me their resume. If I'm interested, I want to look at it. Now! I don't want to have to email you and ask you to send it through to me. Always be proactive and make the job of the person on the other end of the email as easy as possible.

While I'm not a fan of gimmicks or over-the-top applications with twenty-plus pages (honestly, who has the time?), it never goes astray to include something a little bit different to help you stand out from the pack. A beautifully edited, well-presented application with a hint of personality always stands out.

It also always pays to do your research and anticipate the employer's needs. I'll give you some examples.

I once had an applicant courier me a pair of sneakers along with her application, and she included the line 'I would love to be in the running' at the top of her cover letter. It certainly caught my attention! It was also a clever way to tie in her key message with the gift she sent me—which, as publicists, is obviously something we aim for when we do a media send-out. She wasn't quite the right fit for the job, but I do remember her application out of the thousands I've received over the years, so it goes to show it really does pay to think creatively.

When I first started Sweaty Betty PR, we predominately looked after fashion clients. And while we also looked after some beauty and lifestyle clients, Sweaty Betty was known for being the go-to fashion agency. However, in around 2012 we started taking on a few hospitality clients. It was an exciting new opportunity for me, even though I had zero contacts in hospitality media and not much more of an idea about how to do PR for pubs and restaurants.

While we were subtly shifting gears as an agency, every single job and work experience application I received came from hopefuls who told me how much they loved fashion, how fashion magazines were their bibles and how they adored expressing themselves through their fashion. It was fashion overload!

Now, there was nothing necessarily wrong with this. If anyone knows the value of a killer black frock and sexy heels, it's me! It was just that every single applicant was basically telling me the same thing.

One day I received a work experience application from a girl who told me she had a degree in communications and now, just because she loved it so much, was doing a degree in food writing and food marketing. She commented that she had noticed we'd recently started working with restaurant clients and expressed how keen she was to learn about hospitality PR. It doesn't take a genius to figure out why her application stood out from the rest. Not to mention, she had also demonstrated that she was paying attention and had done her research before applying.

The moral to the story is be honest about your experience but be unique. Try to think outside the square a little. After all, if you can't sell yourself to me, how are you going to sell your clients to the media?

When it comes to your resume, keep it factual and no more than two pages long. I've shared the following great example of what NOT to do in one of my seminars. It is so crazy-hilarious-bad that I have to share it again here!

A work experience student who was with us for just one month listed us on her resume when applying for another job. However, she claimed that she had been employed as a full-time publicist with Sweaty Betty PR for three years. To top it off, she fraudulently wrote a reference letter and signed it off from me! Really?! How she thought she would get away with it, I'll never know.

A word of warning: employers check referees. A glowing letter of recommendation (even if it is real but especially if it is fake!) doesn't hold much value until it's validated with a phone call. Don't start on the back foot by telling lies or stretching the truth. Honesty is always the best policy. I would much rather have someone who is honest and trustworthy on my team than someone who looks good on paper but turns out to be a liar.

If you do end up securing an interview, be sure to always send a follow-up email to thank the interviewer for their time. Better yet, send a handwritten thankyou card to show how much you appreciated the opportunity. These small gestures don't go unnoticed, trust me. In the age of digital and people living their lives on their screens, receiving a beautifully written note is a real delight.

On the job

Fantastic, you've got the job of your dreams! Now, how are you going to ensure that you keep it, grow, learn and create a career out of it?

First things first. Know your boss's name and how to spell it correctly! It sounds like a no-brainer, right? (I once had a young woman start with me who spelt my name 'Roxie' in emails. I mean, seriously! Was she even awake?) The same thing goes for colleagues or anyone else you meet on the job. Forgetting people's names or spelling a name incorrectly is rude and unacceptable, especially in PR. You need to figure out a way to remember people's names and fast, because you're going to meet a lot of people in the industry, from co-workers and suppliers, to clients and media.

Getting names right is a basic and essential skill in life and business, so work on it if it's a problem for you.

People often look to me for the secret to success, wanting to learn something no one else knows that will fast-track their career. I get asked so often what is the most important characteristic I look for in a staff member. While some may expect to hear that I'm looking for super-high achievers, whiz-kids or PR strategists, what I'm really looking for is someone who really wants it.

I'm looking for a nice person, who works well as part of a team, takes pride in their appearance and is willing to learn. Being a publicist is a teachable skill (for the most part!) but something you can't teach is being a nice person. And you can't force it if someone doesn't fit nicely within the existing team.

I employ people who are company minded; that is to say, that they care about the clients and the business as if they were their own. They take everything to heart and are truly invested in the success of Sweaty Betty PR as a whole.

Importantly, company-minded people are willing to always go above and beyond to get the job done.

Succeeding in PR, or indeed in any career, really doesn't come down to book smarts, the degree or who you know, as so many people would have you believe. There's a quote I often see floating around on Instagram. It outlines ten traits that require zero talent that will set you up for success. These points sum up employability perfectly and are qualities I genuinely value as an employer.

TEN THINGS THAT REQUIRE ZERO TALENT:

1 **Be on time.** Always be on time; better yet, arrive a little early. This demonstrates that you are organised, committed and enthusiastic. There is nothing worse than a staff member who rushes through the door ten minutes late, looking dishevelled and flustered. Honestly, how productive and efficient are they going to be?

2 **Have a good work ethic.** Do your work and do it to the best of your ability. Don't slack off and

hope someone else will do it for you. This may require putting in long hours of an evening; it might mean pitching in to help your colleagues, or simply taking the initiative to complete a task, without having to be asked. You've been employed to do a job and do it well, so approach each and every task with a solid work ethic.

3   **Make an effort.** Don't cut corners or take the lazy route—it always shows. Put 250 per cent effort into every task you undertake, whether it's writing an email, greeting guests at an event or how you present yourself. Effort is always valued and respected.

4   **Project good body language.** This is a big one—your body language doesn't lie. Even if you are really bored or hating the particular event, day or job, don't let it show. So often I see people with their arms folded, standing awkwardly off to the side of a room, shoulders slouched—I'm no body language expert but it instantly puts me off. Stand tall, look positive and, if all else fails, keep busy.

5   **Be energetic.** The energy you bring to your role is tangible, even if you think no one else can feel it. If you're feeling lazy and unmotivated or are in a bad mood, I guarantee everyone else in the office will sense it too. Think about why you want to be there. Wasn't this your dream job? Even if you hate it, think of it as a learning opportunity and realise how lucky you are to have a job. I can guarantee there are a hundred other people waiting to take your place.

6   **Have a good attitude.** Your attitude to your work is everything. Enthusiasm is key, regardless of the task at hand. Show up with enthusiasm, be diligent and help people. Don't ever think that any job is beneath you. If you approach all tasks with a positive, can-do attitude, it won't go unnoticed. Also remember that it is nice to be important but it's always more important to be nice. As well as making you a decent human, being nice to everyone you meet ensures that you leave a good impression. You never know who you might

need down the track, from the barista to the CEO. Most industries are smaller than you think, especially PR, so you can never be sure who will know whom. Plain and simple, having a great attitude and being kind will take you a long way.

7   **Be passionate.** A job worth doing is worth doing with passion. I speak for the PR industry, because that's what I know. This is not a profession to get into unless you are wholeheartedly passionate about it. There is a massive misconception that the life of a PR girl or guy is all air-kissing over champagne flutes. While of course there are some incredible events and opportunities, the vast majority of the job requires bloody hard work. What you don't see on Instagram are the days and weeks of sitting on emails throughout the night and into the early hours in the lead up to an event, the late nights prepping gift bags and the constant need to come up with fresh ideas and content for your clients. Without passion, I believe it's impossible to truly succeed. It's

passion that will get you through the long days, the shitty weeks and even what feel like the worst years (don't I know it!).

8 **Be coachable.** This is a big one for me. One of my pet hates is a new staff member who walks through the door thinking that they know it all already. I literally learn something new every single day. I've been in business for over fourteen years and if I'm still learning, so is the person who has just started. Be willing to learn, be open to new ways of doing things and always listen to those who have knowledge and expertise to share.

9 **Do extra.** No one has ever got ahead in their life or career by doing the bare minimum. Always be willing to go the extra mile. We have a phrase in the office that we use regularly: 'above and beyond'. Always look for ways you can go above and beyond expectations, whether it's with your time, the results you produce, helping others or the little details that turn something good into something spectacular. If you're unsure of what exactly

you could do to help, ask! Ask your employer what you could do to make their job easier. Take the initiative to ask rather than wait to be told. You should constantly be thinking about what else you could be doing to learn, be productive or be of assistance to your boss or team. Don't sit idly waiting for instruction once you've finished a task—there is always something else. This applies in any workplace.

10 **Be prepared.** A few minutes of preparation can make the difference between looking like a complete idiot and being cool, calm and collected. Whether it's getting ready for a client meeting or an event briefing, or coming into the office on a Monday morning having read the newspapers and with a head full of fantastic new ideas for your clients, it always pays to prepare. Do your homework, read or write some notes to refer to. It doesn't have to be extensive, but a little bit of preparation goes a long way.

There is another trait I would add to this list, and that is to be loyal. Loyalty is so valuable yet so hard to find. People think they can get ahead in their career after spending three months in that job, a year in this one, nine months in another. It doesn't work like that. As an employer, I know the time, money and effort that go into nurturing a new staff member. No one wants to hire someone who is merely going to act as a seat warmer for five minutes before the next person walks in to take their place.

Being loyal also means being honest and trustworthy. I have nothing but trust and faith in my team because I know that they are loyal to me and my businesses. If you're loyal to your employer, it will pay dividends.

I'm not naïve enough to think that staff will stay with me forever; not many employees today will hold a job for a lifetime like generations gone by! However, there are ways to leave your job with dignity and respect, ensuring you also leave a great final impression. Leave the workplace smiling and on good terms, even if there was someone or something about the job you couldn't stand; now is not the time. Send a thankyou card or florals to your former boss, just something small to show how grateful you were for the opportunity. Thoughtful gestures that show your appreciation say a lot about you as a person. Also, you never know when you might be back. It has happened!

Stop wishing for it and start WORKING

If you really want to succeed in your career, you're going to have to work for it. No amount of motivational quotes, wishing or dreaming will get you there. You have to be hungry for it and be willing to put in the hard work that it takes to succeed, and that will include learning the business inside out from the ground up.

All too often I see people start out in PR thinking that they're going to get the shiny, pretty, fun jobs. They expect to walk in the door and be handed the very best clients, as well as an extravagant product launch, complete with cascading florals, canapes and cocktails, that very first week. Sorry to burst your bubble but this is the real world, love. Let's start with the basics, shall we?

When you begin, you will learn to master the fundamentals such as: how to email correctly (more to follow on that later); how to pack, address and send out the mail and courier deliveries the way we do it; and how to display clients' products correctly. Remember, nothing is beneath you—even the most mundane of tasks such as emptying the rubbish, which I still do if I have to! You are being paid to do a job and that job is what your employer tells you it is. Trust the process and believe that everything is done a certain way for a reason.

I once heard a quote along the lines of 'how you do anything is how you do everything' and I think it is so true. Think about it: if you scrappily pack a product sample and it arrives crushed and damaged, which certainly won't make a good first impression, then why would I trust you to execute a media-worthy event? Take pride in everything that you do and, in time, the bigger, more exciting jobs will come.

In short, if you really want it, you're going to have to stop just wishing for it. Don't ever think someone has become successful because of luck.

Luck very rarely has anything to do with it. If you want to invite 'luck' into your career, embrace the opportunity to learn at every step of the way. Do every single task to the very best of your ability. Every time. Always be open to instruction from your superiors and ask questions if you're unsure. If you put in the hard work and combine it with the right attitude, you will succeed.

Always keep in mind that being employed is a privilege, not a right. No one is required to hire YOU for a job. All too often I have seen people take their job for granted or expect their employer to promote them, reward them with a bonus or give them a pay rise after a certain amount of time. You're not entitled to these things. Ever! You earn them, and those who work hard over an extended period of time will be rewarded.

Always be grateful for the opportunity to learn and to be employed, and remember that if you don't want your job, there are at least 150 other people who would give anything to be in your position! If you're not going to work hard and appreciate it, step aside and let someone else have that opportunity.

CHAPTER 2

BUSINESS

Dreaming of starting your own business? Perhaps you already have and you're looking for inspiration and insights to take it to the next level? I get so many emails from aspiring and new entrepreneurs who want advice and guidance. I certainly don't consider myself a business coach but I always take the time wherever possible to share what I have learnt with anyone who asks.

There are no secrets when it comes to success. It really all boils down to hard work, perseverance and determination. It's just a matter of how hard you're willing to work for it. There are, however, a few tips that I believe are relevant to all business owners, regardless of your industry or area of expertise.

You are going to work harder than you've ever worked

These days, everyone wants to be an #entrepreneur. Instagram makes it look very enticing: 'Be your own boss!' 'Work from anywhere.'

Images of people with their laptop sitting by a pool on a tropical island have become synonymous with the entrepreneurial lifestyle. Carefully styled flat lay photos shot from above complete with a green smoothie in a coconut, sunglasses and a passport tend to feature quite frequently as well.

I can see the appeal. The concept of working for yourself sounds like you can rock up to the office whenever you please, take a day off when you fancy and enjoy long lunches on Fridays. Well, that may be some business owners' experience, but it certainly isn't mine! Nor is it the experience of any other successful, goal-crushing entrepreneur I know.

If you need to know anything before you start your own business, know this: in no other job will you ever work as hard as you do when you work for yourself. There are no sick days, no taking your foot off the accelerator and certainly no hiring staff and thinking they're going to do all the hard yards for you. It simply doesn't work like that.

I'm not trying to discourage you from pursuing your dream. Encouraging and inspiring you to do just that are the reason I wrote this book. However, I'm all about being frank. The reality of life as a business owner needs to be shared just as much as all the highs. It's hard labour, day in and day out, often for little or no reward for a long time. There is no finish line: only the next, bigger and better opportunity.

There will be sleepless nights (or years of running on four hours of sleep a night, in my case), challenges, clients who don't pay their bills, bad press, staff who leave you high and dry, rumours, frustrations and failures.

As long as you're prepared to put in the hard graft, dust yourself off when you make a mistake, get back up and just keep going, then you'll have what it takes.

There is no such thing as failure

Okay, this may be an overstatement. Sometimes things do fail. It's life and it happens. How you respond to the failure, however, is what counts. Especially when it comes to business.

Personally, I decided to remove the word 'failure' from my vocabulary right from the start.

Launching a PR agency at 24 with no back-up plan meant that failure simply wasn't an option. It HAD to work. That certainly doesn't mean there wasn't a lot of trial and error, though! I've made my fair share of mistakes and many of them have been well documented in the media. I could have easily thrown it all in, on numerous occasions, but I was determined to keep on going. I've always been driven to succeed, and it should come as no surprise, I'm sure, to learn that I hate to lose.

Rather than see a failure as a problem, I see it as an opportunity to learn. If everything turned out perfectly all the time, then we would never push ourselves beyond the limits of what we thought possible. To this day I am making mistakes and learning and tweaking the way I do things.

I believe this is the most valuable lesson for any entrepreneur: don't be afraid of making mistakes. Always look for the opportunity to learn and refine your products, services or in-house procedures. Through failing, learning and trying again, you will become a better business owner, a better employer and, ultimately, more successful than those who are too afraid to try anything new for fear of failure.

Find your inspiration

People often ask me who my biggest inspiration is when it comes to business. Honestly? It would be my mum, Doreen. From a young age she instilled a strong work ethic in me and is a truly brilliant businesswoman. However, when it comes to famous entrepreneurs and the world's super successful businessmen and women, I'm honestly not inspired by them to succeed.

For me, inspiration comes from within. At the end of the day, you need to be the one who inspires yourself to get up and get on with it, even on the days you really don't feel like it. Actually, especially on those days.

By all means, take inspiration from others' businesses and their successes, if that's what excites you, but don't try to emulate them or their path. In business, authenticity is key. Take ideas, concepts, products and services and make them your own. Be bold and always strive to do things differently and better.

Being unique and authentic is vital in business. You need to live and breathe your brand in everything that you do. Whether that's through your logo, websites, social media, communication, products and/or services, there are endless ways to infuse your touch and your inspiration into your business.

If you really consider it, how successful do you think you will be if you try to do exactly what others have already done? Even in reading this book, I hope that you can take inspiration from my suggestions but merge them with your own way of doing things. No one has it all figured out, even the experts! That's why being your own inspiration is so important in my opinion.

You can't expect extraordinary levels of success if something has been done in exactly that way before. Always look for opportunities to showcase your unique flair and style, because that is the secret to creating a successful business. What can you offer that no one else is offering?

Challenge yourself

As a business owner, one of the worst things you can do is to become complacent. You must keep learning and challenging yourself. Complacency is laziness and it's the greatest threat to creativity, inspiration, performance and success.

Imagine if I had simply stopped challenging myself once Sweaty Betty PR had 120 clients. I wouldn't have started The Ministry of Talent, Pixie's Bows or Social Union, and I wouldn't be writing this book.

This doesn't necessarily mean you need to add another university degree to your office wall, although if that lights your Diptyque candle, go for it! Learning can be anything and everything, from attending seminars (I hear that 'In Conversation with Roxy Jacenko' is a good one!), reading everything related to your business you can get your hands on and keeping up with the news in your industry, to searching on Instagram to see how similar businesses are operating internationally. There is always an opportunity to learn; you just have to look for it.

You can't afford to rest and think you know it all. There will always be ways to improve and new things to learn. The world moves at such a fast pace, especially in the digital space. If you're not on top of the next trend, you can bet your competitors are!

Anyone who is truly successful knows that they need to keep challenging themselves. They never think, *I've made it!* Constantly seek to reinvent yourself, stay fresh and at the top of your game. This will not only keep you inspired but also ensure you stand out from the pack.

Look for ways to improve, diversify and enhance your experience, offerings, services or products. Real success comes from years of trial and error, challenges and daring to do more. Even when you think you've made it, keep going! Innovation is what sets the truly successful apart from the mediocre.

Think BIG!

When it comes to owning your own business, think BIG! Don't settle for second best. Take risks, be adventurous, be ambitious and don't be afraid to stand out.

Once upon a time you may have been able to start a business and cruise along on autopilot without really needing to change much. I think those days are over, especially from a PR and marketing perspective, but also across all industries.

If you're not willing to adapt your business to meet the ever-changing needs of consumers or aren't able to spot trends and pivot your business direction accordingly, you'll get left behind. Being closed-minded or nostalgic about the way we used to do things just won't cut it in today's ultra-competitive and often global marketplace.

Rather than seeing this as an insurmountable challenge, think of it as an incredible opportunity! Now is the time to think big, more than ever before. The future will also open up endless possibilities and new chances for you to grow your business in ways you've likely never even considered.

Thinking big is about ensuring your product or service is memorable for all the right reasons. You don't have to be the next Tesla or Apple! Thinking big can apply to the smallest of details that make all the difference—from writing thankyou cards by hand to each customer or creating customised place settings at an event to personalising products to make them one of a kind.

Look at your brand from the perspective of an outsider. How do they perceive it? Is your offering unique? Is your service next-level? How do you ensure your brand is front of mind?

(I want to make a sidenote here and stress that regardless of whether you sell physical products or services, your business is a brand. 'Brand' doesn't only refer to product, which is a common misconception I've noticed among entrepreneurs. Your brand is you, your employees, your service and your physical products, if you offer them; it's also your website, your social channels and content, your office or store; it's your communication style, even the way you answer the telephone. All of the ways people interact with and experience your business are your brand.)

Thinking big is about ensuring that all these elements of your brand exceed expectation and over-deliver—every time! It's about infusing each of these touchpoints with your brand's exclusive style. Thinking big is also being willing to evolve your product offering or elements of your brand to ensure your business stays relevant. Don't be the business that follows; always aim to be the business that leads and creates a trend.

Stagnating your brand's evolution is perilous. I believe it's the riskiest thing you can do in business. It's far better to take the other kind of risk and dare to do things differently! Never rest until the job, service or product is perfect, and even then never stop looking for ways to improve and grow.

Take opportunities that are presented to you— maybe it's a collaboration with another business in your field or with an artist. Perhaps it's hosting cooking classes to complement your café offering. It may be creating a pop-up experience for your customers when your brand is ordinarily exclusively online. Quite literally, the sky is the limit, unless you're looking to expand into space à la SpaceX or Virgin Galactic!

The opportunity may even come from creating an entirely new business. Often it's related but, in many instances, the idea or opportunity for a new business comes from keeping ahead of trends in your industry and business in general. I'm sure Sir Richard Branson wasn't thinking about owning commercial planes, gyms or rockets when he launched Virgin Records!

If the opportunity is there, even if you don't know how to execute it, just pursue it. You'll find your way through. No matter what industry you're in, if you've got a dream and a gut feeling about what will be successful, then go for it.

Several years ago, I started noticing the trend of social media influencers and the incredible power they had as 'media' in their own right. Dealing with influencers on a daily basis, I saw a gap in their management and business processes. Many of them were inundated with requests from brands and companies but unable to effectively manage the volume of inquiries. They were also struggling to strategise their relationships with brands from the perspective of building their own brand and business.

I realised this was a gap I could fill by offering a one-of-a-kind digital influencer and creative talent management agency, and The Ministry of Talent was born. Did I know back then how to run a digital talent management agency? Ah no, not really! It was the first of its kind in Australia and I was effectively creating a new business niche. However, my instincts told me that this was going to be the next big thing and that the role of influencers in PR and marketing was only going to grow. I took it one step at a time, grew the agency talent by talent and learnt as I went.

The Ministry of Talent now represents some of Australia's most influential bloggers, designers, illustrators, make-up artists, stylists, photographers and social media personalities. Our stable of influencers have collaborated and worked with some of the world's most recognisable brands, creating incredible content, events, imagery and conversations with their followers. While I could never have foreseen the exact way that The Ministry of Talent has grown and unfolded as a business, I knew that the opportunity was ripe for the taking. As I always say, 'Don't think. Do!'

Starting your own business

First things first: start your business with a solid foundation.

Looking back at naïve, inexperienced, 24-year-old me, there are a few things I would tell her if I could. I'm certainly not one for regrets, but with the benefit of hindsight I would offer newbie businesswoman Roxy some tips! Take it from me—it's best to do what I'm about to tell you right from the start.

Get clear on your business idea

If you're trying to be all things for all people, you'll end up being of little value to anyone. I knew from the moment I started doing PR that it was my 'thing'—my gift, niche, specialty. Whatever you want to call your thing, make sure you get crystal clear on what it is that you do well.

While I had the opportunity to move into other areas early on— by providing additional services for my clients such as digital advertising, for example—they were specialties I really knew very little about. Even though it would have meant more in terms of dollars and business, I declined and stuck to what I knew I could do and do well.

This is not to say don't ever expand your offering, try new things or evolve your business. You certainly can't afford to be complacent. Evolution is vital. However, it's so important to know your own strengths, your market and your services or product offering. Pin them down, define them clearly and get to work!

Don't think, do

So, you've got an amazing business idea. Your vision for your business is as clear as day and you can't wait to get started. Great! Now, what are you going to do? Here's a piece of advice you probably won't find in all the business books. Tear up the to-do list! Better yet, don't even waste your time writing one.

In my experience, by the time you've written down a neat, bullet-point to-do list on your trendy Swedish notepad, you could have ticked five items off that list already!

No one procrastinates more than a person with a great idea. You may think your idea is wonderful, unique and sure to be a success. Well, guess what? Ideas are a dime a dozen, and having an amazing business idea is not going to make you successful. Taking action and actually doing the work (and putting in 250 per cent effort day in and day out) are what separates the successful entrepreneurs from the dreamers and the 'one day-ers'. Put yourself ahead of the pack by simply making a start.

So often I see people getting so caught up in organising, planning and prioritising, they're never actually sinking their teeth into the real work. Don't overthink it; stop evaluating your priorities. If it's your business and it's work-related, it's always your priority! Stop talking about how busy you are and how much there is to do. Just make a start.

If you're honest with yourself, you know exactly what needs to be done right now. You don't need to create an elaborate plan to get through your work. Put your head down, grit your teeth if you have to, and start ploughing through your tasks.

Back-end operations

When I first started Sweaty Betty PR, I used to invoice my clients in Word. Yes, you read that correctly: Microsoft Word! I didn't have a formal system in place for chasing debtors and keeping track of payments. Debtors list? How would I have generated one of those in Word?

While it may seem like an unnecessary expense when you start out, getting professional help when it comes to accounts, legal contracts, tax and the general back-end operation of your business is vital. These days there are also a host of small business accounting apps and programs to help you keep track of invoices, expenses and debtors. However, I still firmly believe that it pays to have a professional check out your set-up and systems right from the start. It's vital to ensure you're not missing anything. Do this from day one and you'll save yourself a world of struggle and possibly tens of thousands of dollars. Trust me!

Once you have a solid account-management system in place, it will enable you to check in on the financials regularly. Don't stick your head in the sand, cross your fingers and hope for the best. It may feel like you're raking in money with all the invoices you're sending out, but unless your customers are paying their bills on time, your cash flow may be in tatters. How will you pay your staff? How will you pay the rent? Check in once a week to see how the numbers are stacking up and put systems in place early to monitor and manage debtors.

Additionally, having the correct systems in place will enable you to monitor your performance over specific time periods. You can compare your turnover from one year to the next and, based on those numbers, set specific business goals to achieve in the coming year.

While I'm not one for creating hard-and-fast business plans, I do like to check in to see how my businesses are performing. If there isn't growth from one year to the next, I can investigate why, make any necessary adjustments and move forward with increased drive to make it happen.

Failing to monitor your business financials is a plan to fail. Set up your foundations from the get-go and then you can get down to the real business of doing what you do best.

Systems

My very first job, while I was still at school, was at McDonald's. One of the biggest lessons I learnt from my time there, aside from how to collect tonnes of business cards while working on the drive-through, was the value of excellent business systems.

From the most mundane of tasks, such as drawing up the toilet-cleaning roster, to the most important, such as cooking the French fries for the correct amount of time, everything had a specific process and procedure. Nothing was left to chance and that ensured consistency, which was replicated time and time again. Even as a distracted high-school student, I could see that this was how a successful business should be run.

This is how I now operate my businesses. From day one I have built Sweaty Betty PR and subsequently The Ministry of Talent, Pixie's Bows and now Social Union upon precise, clearly articulated systems. Of course, they have evolved over the years, and there has been a lot of trial and error. However, I can't stress how important it is to have a system in place for all your process work in order to ensure repeatable, consistent outcomes.

Whether it's the way we pack, label and send out post, respond to email enquiries, answer the phone, process payments or manage a guest list and RSVPs, there is a set, specific process that informs the way we do it.

Even packing a gift bag has a system. Our gift bags are just as talked-about and just as photographed as the events themselves. Why? Because they are executed flawlessly every single time, right down to the way the bow is tied.

Anyone can do a good job most of the time. But the secret to doing an excellent job every single time, especially as your team grows, is having those systems clearly defined and adhered to. It takes the guesswork out, sets the standard and formalises the benchmark of your expectations.

No matter what business you're in, the key to success is being able to adhere to the same standards time and time again. Be consistently excellent and you will make a lasting impression.

Your team

Having a great team around you is imperative to success. It has taken me fourteen years to build the amazing team I have around me now. They're like family. It hasn't always been this way, though. Over the years I've had more than my share of misfits walk through the door!

Without doubt, I would say that the most challenging aspects of evolving as an entrepreneur have been finding the right people and constantly driving my business. As the founder and director of four companies, I'm still hands-on with each team member every single day.

Getting the staffing mix right is crucial. The reality, though, is that the trial and error involved in finding the right people can be costly. Hopefully, through learning from a few of my mistakes and lessons, you can hire the right people sooner rather than later. When it comes to HR, the 'human' element means that it's far harder to perfect and systemise the hiring process in the same way you can with other business processes. Be prepared to invest the time to find the right people for you and your business.

Each and every staff member will bring their own strengths and unique ideas to the team. However, it is important to find people who are willing to learn to work in your business with the same drive and enthusiasm as you. You can't physically be everywhere all the time, so you need staff who know exactly how you operate. I work a client's business like it's my own. Their success is my success. I want to hire people who share this commitment and attitude to their work.

When hiring, I interview two or three times. I learnt this from my mum. She has always said that anyone can bluff their way through one interview, but if you get them back a second or third time, it's more likely that their real personality will shine through. This is what you're looking for. See how they handle pressure, what drives them, how committed they are.

Ultimately, you can train for skill sets, but you can't train for personality or work ethic. If you're unsure about what traits to look for when hiring, look back over the 'On the Job' section in the Career chapter.

I've hired people at all stages of their career, from interns who started work experience with me when they began their university degree right through to senior publicists with years of industry experience. Some people may find this hard to believe, but I've actually had the most success with those who have started with me as interns. Not the senior publicists. When a university student starts working with me part-time, I am able to train them from the ground up in the way we do things at Sweaty Betty PR. They don't come with ingrained habits or preconceived ideas about the way things should be done.

Although every industry is different, be open to employing people without direct experience in your industry. While I believe work experience is very important, it's also important to hire people who can learn new things, have the ability to handle competing priorities and work to a deadline, know how to hustle, have a good work ethic and professional workplace standards, and can function as part of a team. The most qualified and experienced candidate may not necessarily be a good fit for your existing team, and that is far more important than their credentials.

If you have hired a staff member and they're not cooperating and performing well within the team, then it's crucial to act quickly. Within my businesses I have zero tolerance for drama. If there is someone upsetting the applecart, I will not hesitate to remove them from the environment. I don't see the point in distressing my loyal, dedicated staff through trying to appease one person who is never going to fit well within the company culture. As a business owner, don't be afraid to step in and take action. A harmonious team is a productive team and, personally, I won't stand for anything less.

Be a leader

I'm very open about how much I push my staff. It's not without reason, though, since I feel it is my duty to ensure that they are performing at their best every day. This is important not only for their professional growth, but also for my clients. Clients don't come to me for substandard results and I don't accept substandard performance from my team.

Do I micromanage new staff to ensure that they're doing their job correctly? Yes, I sure do. It takes time to learn how we operate and as a business we can't afford to make unnecessary mistakes. Sometimes you only have one shot to get it right.

Not only are new staff representing your business but, in the case of PR, they are also representing your clients. First impressions are vital, so if that means micromanaging staff when they're learning something new to ensure it is done correctly, then so be it.

I've made a commitment to be 100 per cent hands-on when it comes to leadership. I work with my team, not above them. Even in the physical sense, I sit with my staff. At one point I sat in my own separate office, but I realised that I was not immersed in the team and ended up losing touch with what everyone was working on. I still have a very lovely private office; I just don't use it! By sitting with my employees and working as part of the team, demonstrating how I expect them to work and driving everyone to perform at their best, I am leading by example.

Never think that you are above anyone or any task. Even as a manager or business owner. Your attitude and approach to work are infectious and will set the tone for the entire team. I'm often the one in the back of the truck unloading goodies to hand out at one of our famous Bondi Beach takeovers! If I expect my staff to do it, I have to be willing to do it too.

There have been plenty of articles written over the years about 'what it's really like to work for Roxy Jacenko'. I make no apologies for demanding a lot from my staff. Am I a hard boss? Yes. Am I a fair and generous boss? Yes. If you are willing to learn, work hard and take direction, then stay and enjoy the ride. If you don't like it and think you know better than everyone else, then leave. It's really that simple. The way we operate as a team and how I lead as an employer are what has enabled us to build an incredible staff and four businesses.

Sometimes as an employer you need to be ruthless. Not everyone is cut out for every job. Ultimately, you are doing your team, your business and the staff member in question a favour by letting someone go if it's not working out. This isn't about being unfair or not giving someone a fair go; if their behaviour and standard of working are letting down the whole team, it's your duty to manage the situation swiftly and appropriately.

Go above and beyond

Good enough is never good enough. Why would you simply meet someone's expectations when you can blow them away? What kind of satisfaction has anyone ever experienced from doing an okay job?

While the answer seems obvious, I feel that cutting corners and doing things the easy (code for lazy) way are all too common. Believe me, while you may get away with it for a time, you won't last. It really is a small world, and regardless of what industry you're in, you can't take any business for granted. It doesn't take long for word to spread if you're doing a shitty job!

Sweaty Betty PR has a reputation for being reliable. We are known for doing what we said we were going to do, when we said we would do it. There is a reason we are the go-to agency for countless media outlets when they need something for a story—it's because they trust us to get the job done every time.

My motto is 'Why walk when you can run?' and I mean this both literally (running in heels is one of my secret talents) and figuratively. It applies to all facets of doing business. Why email out a blind-CC, carbon copy press release to 300 media personnel (and get coverage in maybe one or two if you're lucky), when you can send out 20 unique and brilliant pitches to 20 different media outlets and get coverage in all of them?

Why send out a crappy, cheap gloss bag with a poorly tied ribbon, boring press release and a product sample, when you can provide a totally Instagrammable, 3-tiered lipstick-shaped cake that will have everyone talking, eating, enjoying and sharing the moment and, most importantly, the new lipstick? (Okay, not eating the lipstick but everything else.)

I'll tell you why someone would go for the first option: it's less time-consuming, cheaper and less demanding of your imagination and creativity, while ticking the boxes. Don't be that person.

If you're not going to give each and every task 250 per cent of your devotion, attention and eye for detail, why even bother? Business is far too competitive to do a mediocre job, regardless of whether you're in PR, retail, hospitality or whatever your business happens to be. If your clients or customers have given you their trust, time, money and faith that you will deliver on your promises, you must respect that by going above and beyond for them each and every day.

Good old-fashioned business etiquette

I have placed this topic in the Business chapter of this book, but it applies equally to all chapters. Impeccable manners and good, old-fashioned business etiquette never go out of style and are essential for building relationships as well as attracting and keeping business.

Let's start with the basics: please and thank you. How simple is that? It still blows my mind that I even need to spell it out and it never ceases to amaze me how often people forget to use them!

If you ask someone for something, always say 'please'. Similarly, if someone does something for you or gives you something, say 'thank you'. No exceptions and no excuses. This applies in person face-to-face and in email, but especially in email.

If a journalist or media outlet publishes a story about one of your clients or an influencer shares a post featuring one of your brands, always thank them. It's a small gesture that takes no more than two minutes, and yet it lets that person know that their work is valued and their mention is appreciated. Who do you think will be more likely to want to work with you again in the future: the journalist who gets a genuine 'thank you' for their story, or the journalist who gets nothing except a pitch the very next day, as if their last story never even happened? It's not rocket science.

While it's not always necessary, sometimes it's nice to thank media with a hand-written note or a stunning bunch of florals—particularly if they've gone over and above for you. We often do this at Sweaty Betty PR if a journalist has worked on a feature for one of our clients, as a way of showing just how grateful we are for their work.

It's also a nice idea to find out and remember the birthdays of your key media contacts and send florals and a card to their office. Similarly, take note if they receive a promotion or change jobs and send them a congratulatory card and gift. These thoughtful gestures go a long way in building strong relationships with any business contacts, media or otherwise. People always remember how you make them feel, so ensure you do everything possible to make people feel valued and liked. You'll be amazed how much others are willing to help you out if you show them just how appreciative you are.

The art of the email

When a new staff member starts working with me, one of the first things I teach them is how to use email correctly. Allow me to share. When you've never met or emailed the person you're emailing, always address the recipient with 'Dear . . .' Not 'to', or 'hi' or 'hey'. That's just plain rude. Even though it's just email, it is still a business communication. Not a text message to your best friend. Once you've established back-and-forth emails with that contact, of course you can revert to 'hi', but always in the first instance use your manners and start with 'Dear'.

Another golden rule to remember: always address the person by their correct name! This may seem blatantly obvious but you would be amazed by how many people get names wrong in email, even when the person's name is included in the email address. I'm all about speed and working efficiently, but there are times when you need to stop and double-check and triple-check. Sending emails is one of those times!

Don't simply launch into your pitch. Personalise every email. Yes, every single email. I simply won't stand for my staff being lazy and blind-CCing everyone in their address book with the same email. Take the time to know who you're emailing. If you can, quickly scroll through their Instagram and find out something about their weekend. Or perhaps they have recently come back from maternity leave? Ask them how their little one is going. Did they just return from an overseas holiday? Ask them about it.

Again, this small measure takes an extra minute or two of your time but reaps big results. Showing that you are genuinely interested in the person you're emailing will personalise your pitch and make them feel like they're valued—not just a means to getting your story published (or whatever it is you're asking for).

The email doesn't need to be arduous to write or read. Keep it short, sweet and to the point, but always include a personal touch. You'll build stronger and more productive working relationships with your contacts and ultimately become a well-connected, respected and trusted publicist, manager and business owner.

Master your personal brand

There are entire books written on mastering your personal brand, and for good reason! Your personal brand has never been as important as it is now, especially in the age of social media. We are all more exposed and showing more of ourselves online than ever before.

In PR, you represent not only yourself but also your staff, clients and business as a whole. This is not unique to PR, though, and the same principles apply in any business. From real estate to hospitality, hairdressing to floristry, how you present yourself can affect your business enormously, regardless of what industry you're in.

Your personal brand extends from the way you carry yourself in person to your email and online presence—everywhere, all of the time. When you own your own business, you can't have 'work you' and 'downtime you'—the world is always watching.

The key to mastering this is always being genuine, true to yourself and never trying to act like someone you're not. If you act like a different person in different situations, you're not being true to your personal brand. People will get mixed messages and you risk being seen as less than trustworthy. Always be professional, but always be true to yourself.

My clients know that I'm truthful and they know that I will always give them my honest opinion. They also know I swear and call a spade a spade. If it's the truth, it's the truth! I'd rather be known as a candid individual than someone who lies to keep a client happy. My sincerity and frank method of communicating are my signature and part of my personal brand. People don't hire me for a softly spoken approach; they come to me for solid advice and my honest opinion.

Your personal brand also extends to your physical appearance. We all know that the first impression is everything—although, judging by what some people deem as appropriate to wear in the workplace, perhaps it's not so obvious! I don't care how casual you think your workplace is, there is a difference between being polished and casual and being sloppy and casual. You can look a million dollars in a simple white tee, jeans and sneakers. But are your shoes clean? Do you look like you bothered with your hair this morning or have you just rolled out of bed? Are your nails neatly manicured or is the polish chipped and worn? Is your T-shirt pressed and a crisp white, and does it fit you well?

These things may sound trivial to some, but think about it: who would you prefer to hire to look after your brand or to do business with? The person who looks like they literally threw on the first clothes they found on their bedroom floor that morning or the person who clearly looks after themselves, took the time to dress in well-kept, clean clothes and takes pride in their appearance? While it may not always be true, people will subconsciously assume that you are more competent, capable and confident if you present yourself well.

This isn't about dressing in the latest designer clothes, although if that's your style, go for it. I certainly am not one to judge! It's about looking like you care. Heck, even a plumber can look great if they wear a smart uniform and spend some time on grooming in the morning. Always take that little bit of extra time to ensure you are well presented and polished. Not only will you feel better within yourself, but the confidence you project will also be palpable.

Let the haters become your motivators

Take my word for it: if you're successful, you're going to have haters. It's inevitable! Whether it's a family member who doesn't believe in your ideas or journalists who just seem to really have it in for you (hmmm, that sounds awfully familiar), there will always be people who want to rain on your parade.

But no matter how many people want you to fail, you need to use it as motivation to do even better.

For whatever reason, I fire some people up in the media and on social media. Especially on social media! Seriously, you cannot believe how many faceless accounts with zero posts and 30 followers have so many well-founded, constructive comments to make. Or not! It's actually quite comical.

Rather than let these people tear me down or place any kind of doubt in my mind as to whether I'm doing the right thing, I simply use them as motivation to work even harder. I think, *Fuck you. I piss you off that much? Watch me piss you off even more!*

You will never be everyone's cup of tea. Nor should you want to be. If you try, you will water down your unique personality and talents. Trying to be all things to all people will never get you far. Remember the age-old saying, 'If you want to avoid criticism, say nothing, do nothing and be nothing'.

You can't let fear of haters hold you back. Especially when it comes to business. If you're doing something that is new or a little bit different, you have to expect that some people will judge and criticise you and put your ideas down.

It's always interesting to remember, though, that more often than not this criticism comes from people who aren't doing what you're doing. Perhaps it's out of jealousy? Perhaps it's out of ignorance? I've never quite worked it out, but I've come to accept that there will always be people who want to share their unfounded and uninvited opinions.

My advice for dealing with the haters? Be bold! Say what you honestly think and always tell the truth. It's going to put some people offside. But guess what? That's their problem, not yours. I'd rather associate with people who appreciate my work ethic and approach to business. If you don't like it, take your opinions elsewhere.

The harder you work and the more you succeed, the more the 'haters gonna hate'. Personally, I've never been one to let this deter me. Take my approach, and rather than let these people steal your ambition and passion for business, use their negativity as motivation to do even better!

CHAPTER 3

PR

The publicist 2.0

As fast as the media landscape is evolving, so too is the role of the publicist. These days, consumers are very accustomed to instant, on-demand access to entertainment and constant 'newness'. In one sense, consumers are easier to reach than ever, thanks to the internet, social media and mobile technology. Although in another, it's also harder to really speak to them.

The very nature of PR means it is always evolving as a profession. Without a doubt, the biggest driving forces are digital media and the new ways people consume information from countless sources. More often than not from their smartphones. New digital platforms for news and lifestyle inspiration are emerging as fast as they're folding. The print media landscape has undergone a massive shift as a result.

Gone are the days when a simple press release and a product send-out are enough to get results. Gone too are the days when a few mentions in the newspapers or magazines will get coverage for your product or client. The same goes for any one-dimensional campaign, even if it is online—it's simply not enough.

So where does that leave the publicist version 2.0? Firstly, I'll start with noting that I've always been reluctant to use the word 'publicist' to describe what it is we do. It's not about publicity for publicity's sake! I've been more inclined to call myself a salesgirl over the years, because that's essentially what I'm doing: I'm looking for ways to encourage people to spend their last $50 on my client's product or service. However, the vast majority of people, businesses and clients see what we do as forms of publicity and so we are publicists in their mind. That's why everything I'm about to share with you is aimed at the new breed of publicist: the multi-tasking, multifaceted strategist who can style an event with as much aplomb as they can close a deal.

Traditional media is still the Holy Grail of PR, but traditional media coverage is nothing without digital. Just as digital coverage isn't enough on its own without TV, radio, newspapers and magazines.

The way we approach the media changes every day. If we don't adapt, move with the times and anticipate what's new and what will be next, we miss opportunities.

The news cycle is 24/7 and as such that's how we need to be operating as publicists. We can't rely on an 'office hours' approach to get results. We need to be the ones on the other end of the email or the other end of the phone, ready and willing to do whatever it takes, whenever it is required. We need to be taking a proactive and strategic approach while also being ultra-reactive when it's called for. If Justin Bieber is eating chicken and salad in your client's store, then you don't even blink before getting a photographer on the phone and on the way to snap a photo! Time is always of the essence.

In order to remain relevant and ensure we are getting excellent cut-through for our clients, our tactics and strategies need to be constantly reviewed and upgraded to meet the needs of the ever-changing media landscape.

I started Sweaty Betty PR in 2004, the same year Facebook launched. (Facebook wasn't even a thing back then, let alone Instagram.) Never in my wildest dreams could I have anticipated that social media would become integral to my business, or that I would build two distinct businesses off the back of social platforms.

Just imagine if I had turned a blind eye to the changes in the industry and persisted with the old way of doing things. I would have struggled to keep my clients' brands, products and services in the forefront of consumers' minds. Not to mention that The Ministry of Talent and Social Union would not exist.

Consumer PR is all about managing public perceptions, boosting brand awareness, creating desirability and ultimately driving sales. At the end of the day, that's why the client is paying you decent money. It's all about dollars through their till.

These days, the publicist 2.0 needs to be cunning and creative (more on where to find your creative inspiration to follow). Not only do they need to be able to develop a killer strategy—one that includes a mix of traditional PR, social content, guerilla stunts (if appropriate) and events—but they also need to be able to write an incredible pitch, provide the vision for photoshoots, be the creative directors, organisers and on-the-ground crew at events as well as negotiators and deal makers.

The publicist 2.0 needs to be switched on 24/7, with one eye on their Instagram feed, which is a constantly evolving curation of the taste-makers and hottest talent, influencers and creatives from around the globe, and the other eye on fashion, food, lifestyle and news media. They need to have their finger on the pulse of what is hot right now and what will be hot tomorrow.

Sweaty Betty PR and The Ministry of Talent are industry leaders because we don't follow trends; we anticipate and create them. This is also the approach I have taken in creating a distinct and separate social media content creation and management agency, Social Union. I anticipate what will be the next big thing and jump on the opportunity as soon it presents itself. This is exactly the mindset that the publicist 2.0 needs to have.

'How can I set a new standard and do things in a way that is intriguing and irresistible?' The publicist 2.0 never stops thinking about their client's needs. They are forever seeking exciting, original ways to ensure their products, services and venues are at the forefront of consumers' minds.

Excellent PR is all about channelling effective communication—written, visual and experiential—to drive awareness, desirability and ultimately sales.

The publicist 2.0 is a dynamic communicator, one who is a master at using various mediums and platforms to generate talkability. They are also a skilful negotiator who is willing and able to close a deal, maximising every opportunity for their clients. Ultimately, the new publicist is adaptable, embracing change and rewriting the rulebook to create a whole new way of communicating that can't be ignored.

PR 101—always do your research

The golden rule of PR is always do your research! I refer to this as 'PR 101', the essential skill that all publicists should master.

If you're looking for a profession where you can finish at 5 pm and then switch off for the weekend, PR is not for you. You must always be alert and on the lookout for opportunities for your clients, seeking unique angles or inspiration. You should always be doing your research. Yes, even on the weekends!

Being prepared and taking the time to read magazines, newspapers, websites and blogs, and keeping up to date with the influencers of the moment are essential for PR success. In order to ensure your pitch is relevant and newsworthy for the media, you need to know media outlets inside out, including their audience, style and other stories they've published that are related to your pitch or similar.

In order to build a relationship with the media and influencers, you need speak to them individually—remember the lesson on email etiquette back in the Business chapter? It's so important to know their preferences, their position, the publication and the way it's evolving and changing. Doing your research will give you some context from a professional standpoint and also enable you to ask them questions that make them feel like you care—how was your weekend away in the Blue Mountains? How's that adorable new puppy of yours? Everyone likes to be treated as an individual.

Research is also super important when engaging influencers as part of a campaign. The influencer needs to make sense for the client and their product, not be selected purely because of their follower count. Research is essential to discover their preferences, style and preferred way of engaging with a brand or product. (We will cover working with social media influencers in depth in the Social Media chapter.) I see far too many companies failing to do their research when it comes to influencers—they're the new media, so treat them accordingly.

Taking the time to do your own research is also vital as a matter of courtesy. Spending five minutes before sending that email or sending that invitation could make or break a relationship.

A great example that comes to mind happened several years ago. We received a personalised invitation for a client and her mother to attend a

Mother's Day morning tea less than one month after her mum had passed away. While of course it's impossible to always know these things, on this particular occasion the mother's passing was quite public and a quick check of Instagram (or in fact simply paying attention and knowing who it was they were inviting) would have alerted them to this. This insensitive incident, where the timing was way off, could so easily have been avoided.

The press release is dead

If you've performed your due diligence and researched the media outlets that you want to get your client coverage in, then you will know just how unique each media platform and its audiences are. This is why the 'press release', as many old-school publicists know it, is dead. How can a generic, two-page release be relevant, interesting and on-target for two hundred different media? It's impossible.

To me, this is so obvious! You need to have the foresight to stop and think: is this appropriate, is this useful, is it interesting and relevant, are there any conflicts of interest? If you don't know for sure, do your research.

I started saying that the press release was dead when I first opened Sweaty Betty PR because I didn't have the book smarts or attention span to write one and because the industry needed a shake-up! In my opinion, it was crying out for a makeover. Going for a one-in-a-hundred chance of securing a media placement off the back of a boring press release was simply not my style.

With that in mind, I created 'news snippets': shorter, sharper and far more enticing overviews of the products, services and events I was PRing. They broke every rule of the 'traditional' press release, including the formatting. Essentially, they were beautiful to look at and irresistible to read.

Another key difference from the traditional press release was that the news snippets were accompanied by strategic and thoughtful pitches, each unique to the media outlet and journalist to which they were being sent.

Inspire the journalist with a one-of-a-kind idea

or angle. Give them something that makes writing a story so easy that it's impossible to say no. Importantly, demonstrate to them that you have thought about the pitch, and haven't just gone through the motions. Show them that you know their magazine, newspaper, website, platform intimately and that you 'get' their audience. After all, if it's of interest to their audience, it will be of interest to the journalist.

Journalists want to write the story or produce the TV segment that people can't help but want to read or watch. Make them say, 'Ohhhhh, that sounds good. Tell me more!'

In short, the press release of old is dead. Sending relevant and interesting information is still important, however. How else will the journalist get all the details? It's just that the process has had a major upgrade. At Sweaty Betty PR we have continually refined and polished this process over the years and to this day that is how we operate.

And remember, the press release is just the beginning. It's the pitch and the follow-up that will get the results.

Pick up the phone

Even if your email pitch and news snippet are fresher than Dior's latest cruise collection, sometimes it's just not enough. Regardless of your snappy subject line and on-point imagery, there is so much noise in the inbox of media that you are going to need to take it one step further if you want results.

One thing that infuriates me today is people's aversion to the phone. As in, using a telephone the old-fashioned way—for making calls! I hate the phone as much as the next person when it comes to social calls. PLEASE don't ring me—I'd much rather you just sent a text! However, from a business perspective, the person who closes the deal is the person who picks up the phone.

You can't always close a deal on email. In fact, emailing should only be seen as the initial point of contact. Follow up with a call. Think about it: if you've got your contact on the other end of the phone and you're asking them if they can run a story on your client, don't you think it's going to be a hell of a lot harder for them to say no? It's easy to say no in an email, but I think we can all agree: it's much harder to say no over the phone.

Email has made publicists lazy. They think they can fire off an email and consider it 'job done'. I don't consider it a job well done unless the results speak for themselves. That is why I am always reminding my staff to pick up the phone. Be friendly, be genuine and be helpful but always look to close the deal.

Another proactive way to build your relationship with the media is to do a call-around. Once every few weeks or months, depending on the outlet, phone your contacts and ask them what they're working on. Perhaps there is a story that they're researching and your new client fits the bill perfectly. Ask them what they need and what you can do to make their job easier.

Everyone is expected to do more with less these days, especially in the media. Therefore, it makes sense that if there is anything that you can do to personally assist someone, they're bound to be appreciative. It will also put you on the front foot for upcoming stories and ensure that you and your clients are forefront of mind when it comes to placements, comments in news stories and feature articles.

Live your brands

I'm often asked what it is that I look for when taking on a new client. I'm in the very fortunate position of not having to go out and pitch for business. In fact, we turn away more potential customers than we actually take on as paying clients. There are two reasons for this.

Firstly, I've learnt that quality is better than quantity when it comes to clients on the books. At one point I had almost 170 brands and it became near impossible to manage them the way I wanted to. I couldn't say no to anyone and ended up taking on brands that none of my staff wanted to PR because they didn't like the product—so I ended up personally looking after them. Needless to say, having that many clients soon got out of hand. While it may sound like a money-making machine, there were so many overheads and so much to keep track of, it actually wasn't making great financial sense to continue in that fashion.

The second reason I turn away potential clients is that I refuse to take money from someone unless I know I can get results. In my opinion it's not ethical to take someone's money unless you genuinely believe you can deliver for them. How do I determine if I think a product will get results and cut-through?

When considering new clients, I think about whether I like the product, service or venue. (If you don't genuinely like something, it makes it very hard to PR it.) Can I see potential for it? Would I personally use it? Does it fit nicely within the existing stable of clients? I also think about whether their products or services have potential and desirability in the market.

One way I can tell is by gut feeling. (You'll get this a lot in business, PR or otherwise. Don't ignore it.) I can see potential from the moment I open a website, lookbook or product information pack because I get goose bumps. Instantly my mind ticks into overdrive and I'm flooded with ideas for how we can PR them. I'm inspired and delighted. Believe me when I say that this enthusiasm and excitement translate through into the work we do and our pitches—they're contagious! This is what I mean when I say 'live your brands'. You've got to genuinely love your client's offering and treat it as your own.

On the other hand, when my gut feeling isn't good, then I am always honest and truthful. While I'm sure I've offended my fair share of potential new clients, I'd rather tell them the truth than lie to them, take the retainer fees and then not be able to produce the results. Remember, you can't fake authenticity. It affects everything you do in business.

Another question I ask when considering whether or not to take on a new client is do they have good distribution? By this I mean, do they have a solid network of retailers? Do they have physical stores, a café or a restaurant? If they are an online retailer, do they have a well-presented, easy-to-use online shopping facility that makes for a hassle-free shopping experience? Do they have the capacity to handle increased demand for their product or service? There is no point in securing PR if there isn't an accessible way for consumers to get their hands on the product.

If the answer is 'yes', then we are ready to discuss working with the new client! If not, then I give them my honest opinion about their distribution. I tell them that I don't think their brand or offering is ready for PR and to get 'XYZ'—whatever a suitable benchmark is for that particular product or industry—in place before spending any money on PR. There is no point enticing and encouraging people to buy something if they are not going to be able to find it. It won't leave a great first impression and you'll likely never win their trust again.

PR is for established brands. They can be new, by all means, but everything needs to be ready to go, all systems in place, with product ready to sell. And, ideally, they should have a scalable offering. I wouldn't advise engaging consumer PR for the conceptual phase. That is, you shouldn't be spending money on PR if you don't have a product or service ready to sell or deliver. PR should be done when your offering is AVAILABLE for the consumer: no consumer wants to read about something that they can't actually access.

Where to find inspiration

In order to ensure your brands are relevant and desirable, it's essential to consistently generate creative, out-of-the-box ideas. This is more pertinent now than ever before as the media and influencers are bombarded by PR agencies, brands, products, venues and events vying for their attention and calendar space.

When looking for inspiration, it's important to remember that it's not about simply creating a press send-out or stunt that is attention grabbing purely for the sake of it. It also has to make sense for the product in a way that enhances its appeal.

As publicists, how do we ensure that not only our clients are talked about but their products or services are also? Ultimately, it is not visibility on its own but desirability that translates to sales, which means that you need to be showcasing the client's offering in a way that makes it irresistible across various platforms.

Working in PR is a creative pursuit just as much as a tactical one. I'm often asked how I come up with all the ideas we implement for our clients. From executing full-scale guerilla marketing stunts on Bondi beach to developing stop-motion films for Instagram, my team and I are forever seeking inspiration for our next move. So where do we look?

Inspiration can come from anywhere. Whether it's scanning the world's top fashion magazines every month or going on an international holiday, you should always be looking at new ideas and creative ways of executing events, product send-outs and initiatives. Quite obviously, the internet and specifically social media have changed the game for everyone in this regard. We can all take a look inside the world's most elaborate parties and weddings, watch luxury fashion shows live and view images in real time from the most anticipated product launches. I'm always scouring the internet and Instagram for new inspiration.

It's important not to look at what other PR agencies are doing here in Australia. I don't want to replicate the same ideas that have been seen here time and time again. I want the wow factor that comes from executing something that is new and makes the media sit up and take notice. Not only that, in my mind there is also no point in worrying about what your competitors are doing, let alone looking to them for inspiration. Always look onward, upward and abroad. Remember, think BIG!

I firmly suggest that if you're looking to really stand out, take ideas from all industries, niches and markets and think about how you can combine elements from different campaigns or events and mould them into something unique for your client. What elements of an international beauty launch can you adopt for your client's new restaurant launch? How can you re-create that amazing celebrity baby shower for your client's children's fashion label?

My never-ending quest to stay ahead of the curve when it comes to product and event trends has seen the Sweaty Betty PR team head up some of Australia's most memorable PR stunts. It's also enabled me to PR everything from cars to luxury hotels, restaurants, cosmetics, fashion, toys, bottled water, wedding dresses and even grapes!

While the mix of my clients may appear random, there is actually a method to the madness. Each client's brand, product or service fits nicely within my existing stable of clients, complementing each other and providing opportunities for collaboration. For example, I was once looking after a luxury hotel conglomerate as well as a luxury accessories brand. When we were drawing up travel itineraries for leading travel journalists and travel bloggers, we printed out their travel documents and placed them inside personalised travel wallets that we had had made by our accessories client. Not only was this an additional touch to help their travel experience run smoothly, but it also resulted in sharing and tagging of both clients on social media.

There are countless other ways this can work: your activewear label hosting a yoga morning, with your juice cleanse client providing the after-class beverages; or sending some children's pyjamas along with the Egyptian cotton sheets from your linen client for a bedroom photoshoot. Always be looking for synergies and opportunities to cross-promote your clients. It also pays to be mindful of this when taking on new clients. How does their offering complement or compete with your existing clients?

I actually believe that challenging yourself and your team by taking on clients from different industries can make for even more creative initiatives. It forces you to think differently and prevents you from cruising along on autopilot. You can't PR chargrilled chickens in the same way you PR luxury fashion! You have to stop, take a step back and think about how you can execute activations and send-outs in a different way.

There are no rules when it comes to sourcing inspiration—you can find it in the most mundane or unexpected places. The key is to always be open to it, wherever you are. You don't have to be a creative genius! I'm the first to admit that I'm not a naturally creative person. However, I have the ability to take ideas and concepts and apply them in a unique way that makes them relevant and attention grabbing.

While you may be thinking, *But I'm just not that creative!,* trust me: you can learn to be. You just have to be awake and soak up the world around you. For example, while I was on a brief holiday in Hong Kong I noticed that staff at the Four Seasons Hotel were handing out chilled water in face-spritzing bottles to help guests stay comfortable in the humidity. Naturally, I took a few bottles home (for research purposes!) and together with my mum sent the bottles to China to have them replicated bearing one of my client's logos. We hand-filled hundreds of the bottles with water, placed them in a refrigerator truck and then had some very handsome gents hand out the icy cool bottles to beachgoers at Bondi on a hot, sunny day. Needless to say, they were very popular! And, more importantly, the client's brand name was in the hands of hundreds of potential new clients.

Another example is the beach umbrella activation, which is something I've done for two clients, and on both occasions has worked exceptionally well. I saw branded umbrellas on a beach in Europe and decided they would be the perfect alignment for a bottled water client. This was an opportunity to create a unique collaboration with an artist, who designed the artwork for the umbrellas, while also tying the activation to the environment in a way that made sense: keeping cool in the shade at the beach while enjoying a refreshing bottle of mineral water. The campaign was so successful that those original umbrellas still pop up on Bondi beach to this day, years later!

When thinking about guerilla PR stunts, it's all about the visual spectacle. This creates a buzz and hype at the time of the stunt, but also provides content that can be used across social channels, thereby extending the reach and longevity of the initiative. One only has to look back at pictures of Bondi beach covered in hundreds of identical umbrellas or bright pink, inflatable doughnuts to see how much of an impact these stunts made.

Always look for unforgettable ways to tie the product or brand back into key elements of the press send-out, stunt or event. The product should be the first thing that guests see when they arrive at an event, followed closely by a series of extraordinary details. Whether it's a jar of moisturising cream suspended in the middle of a large ice cube in a dish at a guest's place setting or specially created one-off coffee cups for a particular occasion, it all comes down to details that are sure to make for many Instagrammable moments.

For example, when I launched my second novel, *The Rumour Mill*, we used photocopied pages from the book to wrap the floral bouquets. This was a simple yet effective way to infuse the event with elements of the product and provide guests with a beautiful gift to take away. Naturally, the book itself featured front and centre, but having the pages as part of the floral gifts created even more of a visual impact.

Think about the venue and its colour scheme, location and offering and how they can tie back perfectly with your product. If the packaging for the product is pastel, look for venues that have a similar colour palette and then enhance this with an abundance of florals in the same colour. Perhaps the product has an organic or natural element? Then search for a venue that reflects this in their menu offering. Some of these suggestions may sound obvious, but it's the ability to think ahead and look for as many stand-out opportunities as possible to cross-promote, brand all available spaces and surfaces and create unique synergies that's the real skill.

The same thing goes for media product send-outs. How can you create a visual impact that ensures the recipient can't help but share it on Instagram? Food and florals tend to work incredibly well. Some may call it bribery, but I like to think of it as anticipating people's needs! Who can resist an impeccably decorated cake (that mirrors the product in some way, of course) come the 3 pm office slump? Again, you don't need to be the next Picasso to figure this out. Being creative is all about taking an existing idea and tweaking it in your own way.

In some instances—and I'm always the first to admit this—I take an idea and replicate it. The perfect example from recent times is my Roxy Tan by Skinny Tan launch. From the very start of the campaign I mimicked every detail of the launch of Kim Kardashian's Kimoji Hearts fragrances. I mean, who else am I to copy if not Kim Kardashian? From the 'lovers and haters' Post-it notes list, right down to the chocolate smash cakes with edible mini candies inside, I very deliberately replicated her exact techniques for the launch of Roxy Tan.

While some people were ranting and raving about how unoriginal this was, endlessly tagging their friends in the comments under the video of the launch on Instagram, I was sitting back and smiling, because it had all played out exactly as I had planned. The more comments and tags on the video, the more it had people talking and the higher it was pushed onto everyone's Instagram feeds. The media jumped on it too. Essentially, I got people talking and interested, which, ultimately, resulted in sales.

One question I'm asked about finding inspiration and creating memorable campaigns is 'What's your favourite campaign?' The simple answer is I don't have a favourite campaign or most proud moment, and the reason for this is that I think you can get complacent if you think in these terms. If you think you've already done your best work, what drives you to keep delivering? Like all facets of business, never, ever think that you've reached the pinnacle of what's possible. There are always improvements to be made and opportunities to develop even more newsworthy activations. Keep your eyes peeled and your imagination open to inspiration at all times!

A point to remember when developing stunts, events and send-outs: being loyal to suppliers is wonderful, but it pays to keep them on their toes! You don't want them becoming complacent; make them work for your business instead. This also helps to keep costs competitive for your clients: if a supplier knows they have your business, they could very well charge you above-market rates. But if they know they're competing against a few other suppliers, the costs will be kept in check and they'll go out of their way to impress you each and every time.

Be proactive

Being proactive is vital for PR success. I feel like this goes without saying, but thinking ahead is so important, it's worth a section all its own.

Being proactive applies to timing and also to ensuring that your business and clients are always forefront of mind. Don't wait for the media to come to you. Go to them. Importantly, go to them with a point of difference and before anyone else does.

We often send the media a seasonal gift on certain days of the year, such as Valentine's Day, Easter, Halloween, Christmas and other special occasions. One reason is that they may Instagram the gift but, more importantly, we do this to ensure that Sweaty Betty PR is front and centre. Who knows? They may be working on a story and you'll prompt them to call or email you in regards to one of your clients.

From red roses with gold stems for Valentine's Day, and Donald Trump hairdo-inspired doughnuts for American Independence Day, to handmade floral wreaths for Christmas, our media send-outs are always of the highest quality, have a point of difference and are completely Instagram worthy, as well as being planned, executed and delivered well in advance. Late, crumpled gift bags need not apply!

Being proactive and planning send-outs in a timely manner also applies to client's product releases, events and launches. You MUST be across what they're working on before it happens so that you can be taking action in the lead-up and be ready to launch with a bang. Always think and plan ahead, months in advance if possible. You can't remember that it's Easter the week beforehand and expect to create press-worthy initiatives for your clients with just a few days' notice.

In order to be proactive, it's most important that you communicate with your clients and ask them questions! Always be sure to keep up to date on everything your clients are working on. While it may seem obvious to you that your client would think to tell you when they're working on a new menu or a new seasonal collection, in fact, they may not because they may not recognise the PR opportunity it presents. That's why they've come to you; you're the PR expert.

For example, if your restaurant client is releasing a new menu for summer, anticipate that by asking for descriptions of the new menu items to be sent to you as soon as they're finalised. Arrange for professional photography and styling props if required for use on websites and social media channels. Start working on news snippets to pitch to hand-selected media just before the launch. Perhaps it's worthy of an influencer showcase dinner or lunch? Being proactive will give you plenty of time to plan and execute a strategy that maximises the opportunity, rather than scrambling at the last minute to pull together an impromptu release.

Also think about upcoming media themes that you can workshop ideas for in advance. An example is yearly back-to-school stories—what clients do you have that could fit this theme? We had a grape client that was a really good fit for this particular media theme. Grapes aren't the easiest thing to PR but we came up with the idea of creating the ultimate back-to-school lunchbox: each item in the lunchbox was selected by a paediatric nutritionist and one of those items was a small bunch of grapes. We then packed up the healthy lunches in school-ready lunchboxes and sent them to media and influencers whom we knew had school-aged children. The concept wasn't overly complicated, but with some forethought we were able to execute this send-out with great attention to detail, and it produced outstanding results for the client.

The moral to the story is don't wait for the media to ask you for something. Create the opportunities for your business and for your clients yourself—don't expect them to come knocking on your door.

Dare to be disruptive and take risks

Sweaty Betty PR has redefined public relations in Australia. We are the only agency that the average

Australian has heard of, even if they don't know anything about the PR industry. So why is that?

From the outset, at just 24 and with barely a few months of experience, I've dared to do things differently and refused to adhere to the overused playbook of traditional PR. I've been purposely disruptive in an industry that adhered to some fairly boring rules!

I've also willingly taken lots of risks, some of which paid off and a few of which did not. May I take this opportunity, though, to stress that my risks have not been financial! I don't believe in taking financial risks. The biggest financial risk I take in business would be getting a ticket from the council for $350 when we do a beach activation. But, when the media coverage is worth a million dollars for the client, it's a very small financial risk, and it's well worth it.

The type of risk I'm recommending you take involves your approach to PR and doing things differently from everyone else. The risk is that your stunt falls flat and doesn't work, at which point you try again. The pay-off when it does work? You pull off one of the most memorable PR campaigns your client has ever seen and they are ecstatic.

If the press release is dead and the publicity market is at saturation point, how do we get the attention of media and consumers? How can we stand out as an agency? How can we disrupt the market? These are questions that I ask myself and my team constantly.

To borrow a quote from one of the most masterful businesswomen of our time, Maria Hatzistefanis, aka Mrs Rodial of Rodial Beauty, 'Don't think outside the box. Think like there is no box.'

If I had done things by the book, by thinking just outside the box, then I don't think Sweaty Betty PR would have become a household name. Why would it? There seems to be a new PR agency every other week and competition is fierce. However, by thinking like there was no box (literally, because I didn't even know all the PR 'rules' let alone want to follow them), when I first started, I've been able to disrupt an entire market.

Remember this: laws are made to be adhered

to and rules are made to be broken. You've got to be prepared to bend them a little, and sometimes break them, in order to create something that is really spectacular. Imagine if Steve Jobs had decided not to bother breaking all the rules and making the mobile phone as he imagined it because Nokia had already made one!

I never look for inspiration from my competitors. Don't look left. Don't look right. What they're doing is of no significance. Just keep looking forward. That's where I want to be.

Being disruptive also means continually evolving and asking, 'What's next?' You have to be open to change, forever developing and acting quickly on the new and the next big thing. This also makes smart business practice because you're not putting all your eggs in one basket: you're diversifying your offering and the types of clients you are working with. And, in doing so, you're lowering your risk in a business sense because you've got income streams from multiple sources and industries. If the fashion retail market goes flat, for example, you've still got hospitality and beauty clients. If all the print magazines go out of business tomorrow and traditional PR opportunities are out of the question, it doesn't matter because you've still got expertise in events, guerilla stunts and social campaigns.

Taking risks and being disruptive are my core business strengths. As you're about to learn in the next chapter, nowhere else has taking risks, daring to be disruptive and jumping on opportunities paid off more than with social media.

CHAPTER 4

SOCIAL MEDIA

The rise and rise of social

To say that social media has completely changed the face of PR and business is an understatement. It hasn't re-written the rule book—it's demanded a new one entirely.

No other technology has had such a profound impact on the way people interact with each other and, perhaps more importantly, on the way brands and people communicate. So why is social media so popular and showing absolutely no signs of going anywhere anytime soon?

I believe it is because we all secretly love watching other people's lives! It's like the celebrity 'what's in my handbag' pages in magazines, but on steroids. Everyone loves a stickybeak into others' lives—especially when they're seemingly more interesting, glamorous or downright absurd compared to our own. We are all guilty of it, I'm sure. I know I am!

From a business perspective, social media has levelled the playing field. Where once only the big brands were able to afford to take out a months' worth of full-page ads in the newspapers and glossies, now even the smallest of start-ups can afford to reach audiences of tens if not hundreds of thousands of people for a fraction of the price.

It has also completely changed the nature of PR, not only opening up countless more platforms in which to showcase brands and clients, but also creating an entirely new dynamic: instant gratification.

Where once we had to wait for the likes of *Vogue* and *Harper's Bazaar* to publish their September issues in order to see the latest collections from the runways of New York, Paris, Milan and London, now we can watch the shows live on our own devices.

The brands themselves often stream the shows live on their social channels, while bloggers, stylists and media platforms are incessantly snapping, Instagramming and vlogging every moment from the front row. In fact, these days, by the time Karl Lagerfeld steps out to take his bow on the runway, the world's fashionistas have already started their new-season wish lists.

This instant gratification applies not just to fashion, but also to every other industry as well. Whatever is new, hot and happening, no matter where it is in the world—we want it right now. From food to technology, entertainment to art, the world has become more connected and somehow smaller thanks to social media. It's also created infinite possibilities for creativity and entrepreneurship.

Eva Chen, the ultra-cool director of fashion partnerships at Instagram, has said, 'A picture is worth a thousand words and now a picture can speak to millions of people.' If you stop and consider just how much those small, square images have changed media, communication and business, it really is remarkable.

Think of Instagram, or indeed any social platform, as your personal media outlet to share your ideas, creativity, product and personality, and you soon see that the possibilities really are endless. The following is a round-up of my personal experiences, tips and advice to ensure you maximise social media from a professional perspective.

Choose your medium and do it well

With so many social platforms available and new ones cropping up all the time, it's hard to know where to focus your attention. Instagram, Facebook, Snapchat, YouTube, LinkedIn, Twitter—how do you know where to start when it comes to your personal brand or business?

Too often I see new businesses, and some bloggers, for that matter, start out all guns blazing with a blog, YouTube channel, Facebook account; you name it and they're on it! Soon after, the quality and quantity of the content start to drop off. It turns out that keeping all those platforms updated, fresh and unique is a lot of work!

For me, there is no point in sharing the same content on different platforms. Unless it's a sneak peek to drive traffic from one platform to another. But sharing the same image on Instagram, Twitter and Facebook? What's the point? Your followers aren't following you onto different platforms to see the same imagery, commentary or video.

Quite simply, it's lazy and boring social media management.

Unless you're a large organisation with the capability and resources, such as a dedicated social media manager, my advice would be to choose one or two platforms and do them exceptionally well.

For Sweaty Betty PR, those platforms are Instagram and Facebook. We use Facebook to share image libraries of events and activations, as a digital photo gallery of our work. We use Instagram as our predominant social media platform where we showcase our day-to-day activities and the best imagery from our clients. A quick scroll through the Sweaty Betty PR Instagram account will give anyone a high-level overview of the type of work we do and the type of clients we work with.

While Facebook is becoming far less relevant for me as a business owner, I know there are many businesses out there that rely heavily on the platform. There are also many consumers who expect to be able to find a Facebook page for a business, particularly if it's service based.

Facebook's star rating and review elements can be useful for small businesses. These may change in the future as the role and use of Facebook change, but for now having a Facebook page is vital for many businesses. Take the time to consider your use of and approach to Facebook to ensure that you're not re-posting the exact same content on Instagram!

If your business sells a physical product, then, to me, having an Instagram presence is a must. Instagram is a visual platform and is the ultimate way to showcase your product in a variety of ways, from styled flat lays to it being used or worn. Instagram may not be as relevant for some service-based businesses, so it's always a matter of case by case, and considering whether or not you can continually create relevant, interesting and high-quality content for it.

YouTube is big business for many brands, including individuals who have built entire careers out of showcasing their everyday lives on vlogs. To think that it is now a viable career to film yourself doing your make-up or playing video games, and that you can make a decent income (a remarkable income, in some cases) from it is really quite astonishing! From a business perspective, I would suggest that unless you or someone on your team is particularly good at speaking in front of a camera and/or you've got the resources to create beautifully edited footage from events, launches, behind the scenes or tutorials specific to your product or industry, then perhaps YouTube isn't for you.

Snapchat is another platform that some brands use very well. It all depends on your audience, the content you're creating and whether it is best optimised on Snapchat's unique platform. I've heard of some brands using Snapchat to showcase 'day-in-the-life'-type content from their staff, which can work very well. However, it all comes down to what makes sense for your brand and your offering, as well as what your audience finds entertaining and useful.

Don't waste time and money trying to have a presence on every social platform. More is not more when it comes to social. Think about the reasons you're sharing what you're sharing—don't do it just for the sake of it or just because Kylie Jenner is doing it. The rules don't apply to her! Ask yourself: what does your audience want from you? What do you personally enjoy using and what are you good at?

Remember that on each platform there are experts who have mastered it and optimised it and that because of this, consumers have become accustomed to sophisticated, high-quality content. Don't spread yourself too thin. Choose one or two platforms that work for you, and focus on perfecting them, pushing the boundaries and above all having some fun with it!

How to curate a killer Instagram feed

While there are, of course, countless social platforms, for me as a business owner and publicist, it's all about Instagram. It is the platform I've had the most success with professionally in terms of results for my clients and businesses.

Instagram not only provides excellent cut-through in terms of visibility and brand awareness, but it also increases dollars through the till, which is ultimately the end result we are all looking for. For these reasons, it's the social platform I focus all of my energy on, and it has grown into a thriving side hustle in its own right.

Instagram is hot right now, but that doesn't mean that one day it won't be gone. Instagram could very well be phased out and replaced with a new social platform or medium we can't even conceive of right now. When that time comes and Instagram is replaced by something better, bigger or more powerful, then we will jump on it. Never be afraid to embrace change. For now, though, Instagram is my speciality and my core social focus.

Instagram has given Sweaty Betty PR and our clients a new form of communication that provides a brilliant visual aesthetic. The tech geniuses behind Instagram certainly knew how to create something visually appealing, which is perfect for PR, as well as incredibly simple to use and highly addictive!

Like everyone else, when my team and I started using Instagram, we had no idea how to maximise its potential. Back then, we were all making it up as we went along. Just scroll back to your very first Instagram posts and you'll likely find some great examples of what not to do: blurry pictures, terrible use of filters, tacky borders and inconsistency in styles and themes.

Instagram has come a long way since it launched in 2010, becoming a powerful tool for creatives, brands and savvy individuals who've built careers and hugely successful businesses purely off the back of the platform.

As I mentioned in the introduction, I didn't set out to become an Instagram 'influencer'. I started my private Instagram account when my personal life was starting to merge with the Sweaty Betty PR account, and I wanted to clearly distinguish between the two. When I started my private account, I was sharing a glimpse into my everyday life: candid snaps of my family, days at the office, meals, outfits and holidays. This is essentially what I still do to this day, despite building a following of over two hundred thousand and counting. I haven't drastically altered my approach or tried to present myself as someone I'm not just because I've built a following. I think it's important to remember that people have a pretty low tolerance for inauthentic content, especially now that Instagram has over eight hundred million active users around the world! If people don't like what you're posting or find it way out of line with your 'brand', they will soon stop engaging with you and may even unfollow you.

Everyone wants to know the secret to Instagram success and how to crack the all-important algorithm, and questions on this topic are among the most frequently asked at my 'In Conversation with Roxy Jacenko' seminars. In the process of growing Instagram accounts for my businesses, myself and for my children, Pixie and Hunter, I've learnt a thing or two about what works and what doesn't and I've inadvertently become the go-to social media expert. All because I trusted my gut instinct and was willing to learn on the job!

While everyone has their own opinion as to what works, how to attract more followers and how to increase engagement, the following are my top six tips for Instagram that I use on all the accounts I manage.

HAVE A CONSISTENT MESSAGE

Ensuring that you have a consistent style, voice, tone and filtering style, if at all, would have to be my top tip. Some accounts do this to great effect but they're generally the more artistic accounts. Most importantly, make sure that your account has a consistent, overarching theme, and a clear direction and purpose. If it is a fashion business, make sure your grid reflects this. If someone visits your Instagram homepage, it needs to be immediately obvious what your account is all about.

Don't try to be everything to everybody. Post content that is relevant and real to you. Tell a story with your images that is part of a bigger story for you or your brand. Don't try to be someone or something that you're not. Think about what it is you want to be known for. Are you a subject matter expert, do you have a hobby or passion that you want to share with the world, are you a creative, an artist or a small business owner? Think about what it is that makes you or your brand unique and what would make people interested to find out more. Then make sure that the images you share consistently relate to that.

There is a common theme among the most successful Instagram accounts and that is their style is instantly recognisable—their grids have an 'it' factor. People love new things, but they also love familiarity. You need to give your followers new and inspiring content but in a way that they can come to expect from you.

ENSURE THAT YOUR CONTENT IS HIGH QUALITY

Instagram is all about the visuals. Generally, the caption is secondary to the all-important picture. People now have extremely high standards when it comes to image quality, especially on Instagram. And these days, everyone has a pretty decent camera in their hand at all times in the form of a smart phone. There really is no excuse for a blurry image!

Followers will naturally gravitate towards and engage with beautiful, well-produced, high-quality content. With a little bit of practice and patience, everyone should be able to curate a collection of high-quality images.

DON'T RAMBLE, AND KEEP THE HASHTAGS TO A MINIMUM

There is nothing worse than an essay in your Instagram copy! People go to Instagram for a quick visual hit. They generally don't go there to read long, drawn-out stories and explanations as to why you posted the picture. Chances are they'll keep on scrolling if your image is secondary to some lengthy prose. Keep it short and sweet. Importantly, use hashtags where necessary but keep them to a minimum. Including generic hashtags won't increase your engagement; if anything, it's actually more likely to attract spammy, low-quality accounts.

Hashtags are useful if they're unique to a brand,

campaign or initiative but I personally don't go overboard with them.

BE TRUE TO YOURSELF

Remember that your audience is following YOU! They are following you or your brand because you have something unique to offer. If you start to post generic content that isn't organic and natural for you, you will soon start to lose more followers than you gain. By all means, be inspired by others but don't copy them.

It's impossible not to be inspired by the thousands of talented Instagrammers out there. But it is SO important to create your own unique Instagram style, and put your own twist on things. People will visit your feed to see if they're intrigued and interested enough to follow you, so merely copying others to a tee won't be enough to stand out!

When it comes to sponsored and branded content, staying true to yourself and your personal brand is vital. You can't send out mixed messages or else your followers will see right through you. Only engage with products and brands that you genuinely like and would use. It's a simple decision—do you feel comfortable and like the 'real' you when sharing this product/brand, or are you simply doing it for the money?

POST REGULARLY BUT NOT TOO OFTEN
There's no denying, Instagram is crowded.
In order to stand out and make it into your followers' top feeds, you need to post regularly and consistently to ensure you're front of mind, while also being careful not to bombard your followers with too many posts. I would suggest posting every single day as a minimum, but aiming for no more than two to three posts per day. Don't post merely for the sake of posting; your content and frequency need to be right for you and your brand.

IT'S CALLED 'SOCIAL' FOR A REASON
There is a reason it's called 'social media' and it's because it's been designed for people to be social! It's not meant to be a one-way communication channel. In order to maximise its potential, Instagram, as well as other social media platforms, should be used accordingly.

Instagram is a visual tool for engaging with others who are in a similar field or have similar interests as well as with existing and potential customers. It's about using your brand's visual aesthetic to communicate and interact with others.

Follow other accounts that inspire you or that are related to what you're doing. Leave meaningful comments or reply to people who ask you questions. Tag locations, friends and brands in your photos where relevant—give people the opportunity to find your images and feed. Reach out to like-minded accounts and people where appropriate and look for opportunities to collaborate. This will connect you with a broader audience of people who may be interested in what you have to offer and open the door to endless creative possibilities.

Using Instagram for its intended purpose—being social—unlocks the algorithm and helps boost your visibility. But this doesn't mean being contrived or spamming people; as with everything to do with branding and PR, authenticity is best.

It's important to remember that numbers aren't everything. Having a million followers doesn't mean a thing if you don't have an engaged audience. One loyal and engaged follower is a hundred times more valuable than someone who occasionally skims over your post, and infinitely more valuable than a fake follower who's been purchased! (I don't even want to go into why fake followers and spam accounts are wrong. Just don't go there.) Loyal followers will come when you're just being you. Rather than chasing numbers, focus on generating organic content and engagement first and foremost, and your follower numbers will naturally grow.

Just have fun with it! Instagram isn't meant to be serious. There's no need to force your style or try too hard. I think followers can see through people or business accounts that are trying too hard and posting content just for the sake of it. Create a sense of community and authenticity that will see people commenting on your photos, tagging their friends and ultimately making your feed irresistible.

Treat your followers like the real people that they are. There is nothing worse than people or brands treating their followers like advertising space. Adhere to the social rules you'd follow if you were at a dinner party—be courteous to others' opinions, don't shout at people (you can absolutely detect this even in comments!), don't be rude and only type what you'd be willing to say if that person were right in front of you.

Working with influencers

Bloggers, digital influencers, content creators, taste makers—whatever you like to call them, there is no denying the phenomenal impact of social media influencers. Showcasing their creative talent and lifestyle while working with brands (anything from fashion and beauty, hotels, cars, restaurants and events to destinations, and everything in between), social media influencers have become big businesses themselves.

In a sense, influencers have become the new media. Many boast larger follower numbers than most traditional publications have readers. Instantaneous, adaptable and relatable, influencers have completely changed the way people create and consume content and the way brands communicate with consumers.

Influencers have developed an entirely new marketplace that is constantly evolving and growing. No one could even have dreamt of the job description of an influencer even just ten years ago. We are all still learning and adapting to the new way—myself included!

While influencing is undoubtedly a big business globally, many businesses are still finding their way when it comes to working with influencers, either at all or effectively. I find this to be true particularly for small businesses that are yet to realise the ability they now have to communicate with a larger, more targeted audience than ever before. Even with a small budget, especially when compared to traditional advertising, influencer marketing can have huge impacts for small business.

When I started The Ministry of Talent, I could see a gap between the reach and engagement levels of influencers on the one hand, and brands trying to effectively communicate with their markets on the other. To me, providing a service that connected brands with the right influencer or influencers was a no-brainer. Business owners could see the potential or see other businesses having great success with influencers, yet were unsure how to achieve similar results for themselves. Having worked with countless brands from the perspective of The Ministry of Talent for over six years now, I've learnt some simple tips for what works and what doesn't when it comes to influencer strategy.

While it is tempting to try to align your business with the influencers who have the largest follower numbers, it's more important to consider who really speaks to your audience or market most authentically. Numbers aren't everything. Sometimes an influencer with a smaller, more niche following is more powerful than a mega-influencer with several million followers. It all depends on your brand and your objectives. Who is your desired customer? What do they like on social media? Who do they follow? Who or what influences their purchasing decisions?

It may be a better option for your business to engage five to ten influencers who charge $1000 per post and who speak to your target audience, rather than one influencer who charges $12,000 per post and speaks to a much larger market. Believe me when I tell you that there are influencers in the Australian market who charge that much and more! Looking to hire a Kardashian or Jenner? Best your chequebook can accommodate at least six figures!

Repetition and consistency are what's going to get results, not a one-off post. Think strategically and consider how you can build awareness and desirability through a series of posts from a number of different influencers. That's what will get customers through the door or your online check-out. If you've got the budget for multiple posts at several thousand dollars a pop, then go for it! But don't think you need to have exorbitant budgets to see results; it just comes down to doing your research and thinking strategically.

Look for influencers who would naturally use your product or services. Does it seem authentic for them? Better yet, try to engage with influencers, even those with a modest following, who are already a fan of your brand. They're more likely to want to work with you and it will be a more genuine and organic alignment for them and their followers.

The same rules apply when engaging a creative content maker for a collaboration. A whimsical fashion illustrator may not be the best fit for your classic restaurant or café. And the brilliant food stylist and photographer who is the master of flat lays probably isn't going to capture your launch event in the best possible way, either.

By all means think outside the square—sometimes an unexpected perspective or unusual collaboration can work really well. I'm all about taking risks and breaking the rules! However, think carefully about your objective and desired outcomes. Do you want to spike engagement by posting something out of the ordinary or do you risk being too controversial? Are you looking to build a bank of unique imagery? Perhaps you're looking to enter a new market?

Beware the influencer who willingly accepts your money without taking the time to ask you about your project objectives and learn more about your brand, products and services. Some influencers will accept any paying job, regardless of the brand fit. One day they might be posting about their love of sugar-laden sweets and the next day spruiking the latest detox tea. If in doubt, don't proceed. You'll know when you've found an influencer who feels right and is a good fit for your brand.

If you're a new or small business and don't have any budget for paid influencer marketing, don't be deterred. Often influencers are willing to work in exchange for product or a meal, experience or a service. The key to working with influencers this way is to be honest. Connect with them directly and tell them why you like them and what you love about their social media presence. Explain your service or product and why you think they would enjoy it. You'd be surprised how often influencers are willing to work with smaller businesses. After all, we all love to share a great find with our friends! Never underestimate the power of being genuine and asking someone for their expertise or help. If you never ask, you'll never receive!

CHAPTER 5

LIFE

Sh*t happens

No matter how glamorous someone's life may look from the outside, rest assured that everyone has something going on. Family dramas, problems at work, health issues—we all have them and we are all human.

I try to be as open as possible about my real life in interviews, my seminars and on social media. I don't do it for sympathy or from a place of 'poor me'. I want to tell people the truth and show the day-to-day realities of my life—the good and the bad. There are plenty of people who are in far worse situations than I've ever been in, which I'm very conscious of. I'm simply sharing what is, in the most authentic way I know.

I have struggles just like everyone else. Some of them have been quite life-changing and have played out in the public arena. My husband, Oliver, going to jail for twelve months and then me getting diagnosed with cancer just weeks later are two of the more obvious struggles I've had in recent times.

On the other end of the struggles scale, there are the days when I'm like any other working mum and I'm battling with the kids to get them in bed at a decent time, before jumping back on emails to plough through my work for a few hours.

In 2016, which was undoubtedly the most challenging year of my life, I could have easily thrown it all in. I could have walked away and played the 'woe is me' card. Instead, I took my responsibilities as a mother and a business owner very seriously. I had a duty to my family, my team at work and my clients to show up every day and make it work.

No matter how shit things are, no matter how many challenges are in front of you, you've got to put all that negativity in your pocket and just keep going. If you've made a commitment to do a job, whether as a business owner or an employee, or as a mother, wife or friend, you can't let excuses get in the way of seeing that commitment through.

Realise that everyone has something going on in their life that you know nothing about. We all have problems, big and small. Making excuses, feeling sorry for yourself and letting people down aren't going to improve the situation. Hold you head high, quit the complaining and get on with things as best you can.

Quit the gossip

No one will freely admit that they gossip, yet we are all guilty of it from time to time. Gossiping about your favourite celebrity's latest romance over a latte with your besties, however, is a little different from gossiping about friends, work colleagues and clients.

Don't speak ill of someone behind their back. This applies to life in general but especially in business. How you speak about others when they are not around will say more about you as a person than it will about them. If you have an issue with someone, it's best to address it directly. Not by whingeing and moaning about it to your colleagues.

The best-case scenario when you gossip is that you are left with that icky feeling and are no closer to a solution. The worst-case scenario is that the person finds out about what you said and it blows up, becoming an even bigger issue. Gossiping is not productive, nor is it a becoming trait, so while it can be ever so tempting at times, you've got to keep yourself in check. Loose lips sink ships! Don't go there, it will always come back to bite you.

When you own a business, you're representing not only yourself but also your staff and clients. By all means, be honest and call it how it is—I think it's pretty clear by now that's how I operate! However, there is a difference between calling a spade a spade and gossiping. Be aware of how others may interpret what you're saying and, if in doubt, keep your mouth shut!

Be a decent human

You can have all the potential, ideas and drive to become the most successful businessperson in the world, but none of it will matter if you're not a decent person. How you treat people is just as important as how you balance the books or strategise your next big move.

The old saying is true: if a person is nice to you but rude to a waiter, they're not a nice person.

Just as no job is beneath you, neither is any person beneath you. As you grow and become more successful in business or your career, it's important to remember that you're no better than anyone else. Be nice to people on your way up, because I can guarantee that if you're not, you will see them again on your way back down.

The most successful businesspeople in the world are often the most generous. You may not always see it, but I guarantee that they give generously in terms of their time and resources. Ultimately, you won't be successful or happy in life if you're rude and treat others with disrespect.

If you're successful, people who don't even know you will be the first to judge, criticise and make assumptions about what you do or don't do. Sometimes it's tempting (oh so tempting!) to hit back and prove them wrong. At the end of the day, though, you know how you should treat others and you know whether or not you've done the right thing. Being a decent human isn't about doing it for the 'likes' and public accolades. It's about always doing the right thing, being the bigger person and treating everyone with respect, even when no one is watching.

Be your best

For a long time, I put my health last. It was my lowest priority. I was running a business, looking after two young children, starting a second business, looking after more staff and more clients, and dealing with more dramas. When did I have time to look after myself? 'I don't have time to go to the doctor,' I would tell myself. Until I had a massive wake-up call in the form of breast cancer.

When it comes to my health, I've done many silly things over the years. Barely eating enough to get by or 'eating air', as I call it; taking too many painkillers to get through the tough days; not exercising. I'm certainly no poster girl for the wellness tribe!

However, I've definitely made my health more of a priority in recent times. I learnt the hard way that you're no good to anyone if you haven't got your health. For twelve months from 2016 to 2017, I was subsisting on air. I couldn't think straight. I had zero energy and very little creativity. I was showing up at work but I wasn't there. My work and business suffered as a result.

I now make sure that I exercise three or four times a week. I eat regularly throughout the day, enjoying a balanced and healthy diet most of the time with a few indulgences here and there when I feel like it. Care for a glass or two of Viognier, anyone?

I have a responsibility to my family to provide for them. I have a responsibility to my team to be present and performing at my best so that the businesses grow and succeed. I have a responsibility to my clients to deliver excellent results and to be across everything that is happening in the business. Looking after my health is key if I want to be able to perform at my peak.

Failing to look after yourself isn't heroic. It's stupid. If you don't look after yourself, then you can't perform at your best. Being an entrepreneur or, in fact, anyone looking to get ahead in their career, will require many sacrifices. While I'm definitely still working on my own health, my advice is don't make your health one of those sacrifices.

Forget about balance

Whether you want to start your own business or are looking to excel in your chosen career, there is a prevailing myth, in my opinion, that you should be seeking balance.

Take my word for it. You can forget about balance. What does it even mean, anyway? To me, the term 'balance' suggests that there is some semblance of equality between how much time and effort you put into all areas of your life: work, rest, play, family.

There is no balance when you work for yourself. Yes, you can still make time to spend with your family or to look after yourself. But day to day, your life will be anything but balanced. It's all a matter of priorities. Once you know what they are, you will spend your time accordingly.

Personally, I don't enjoy relaxation in the usual sense. I would rather take care of work emails all weekend than laze by a pool! I enjoy work because I want to set an example for my children and instil in them a solid work ethic. I also enjoy it because I want to drive my business forward and see my team grow and succeed. I don't want to be in a position where I have to wish for anything in my life. I like nice things—what can I say? I want to be able to buy what I want to buy, give my children memorable life experiences and travel to nice places. My husband also has expensive taste but, ssshhhh, I didn't tell you that!

Lounging around and relaxing do not float my boat so I don't prioritise them. But, if that's what *you* love, then go for it. Only you can decide what you want to achieve in life. We all have the same amount of time available to us each day. I'm often asked, 'How do you find the time, Roxy? How do you manage it all?' Well, I don't have a magic time machine that gives me more hours in the day, that's for sure!

My answer is always that I am no busier than anyone else. I just do what I need to do as it crops up, without giving it a second thought. I find the time because I make the time based on my priorities. If you're brutally honest with yourself, you'll know where you are wasting time and where you could add a few productive hours to your day if you really wanted to. I'm not suggesting that you try to survive on four hours' sleep a night (it's a skill, what can I say?), but I am suggesting that you probably spend hours a week aimlessly scrolling through your phone or socialising with people merely out of a sense of obligation.

Success requires sacrifice, make no mistake about it. My advice would be to think about what areas of your life you are willing to sacrifice to create the life you really want for yourself. Stop thinking that successful people are lucky and start realising that the vast majority make their own luck. They are just willing to go without relaxation, play and a social life for a long time!

EPILOGUE

FIND YOUR INSPIRATION

If you're the kind of person who has taken the time to read this book and reached the end, that's a pretty good indication to me that you want to succeed in life. You're already looking to better yourself and expose yourself to new ideas and a different way of doing things. Having that curiosity and drive to find out more and learn is a valuable quality.

Perhaps you've got a big business idea or perhaps you're still at school and burning to get started in the career of your dreams? Maybe you're unsure about what it is that you want to do but you just know that you're determined to be the master of your own success and destiny. You should take comfort in the fact that just by being here and reading these closing pages you're well on your way! Many people never even take the first step but put it in the 'too-hard basket' or the 'I could never do that' category. You're clearly not one of those people!

I'm not the philosophical or reflective type. I'm more of a 'shut up and get the job done' kind of girl! However, after years of fielding emails and, in more recent times, live audience questions about my business experiences and PR tips, I've come to understand just how valuable it is to share your knowledge with others. If I can help just one aspiring business owner make their dreams come true by sharing what's in this book, I will consider it a success.

In writing down my tips and tricks, my biggest motivation was to provide a source of honest, real-life advice, insights and truths about running your own business. I speak about PR and social media from a place of experience. Not everyone will agree with my ideas and suggestions but they have worked for me. The same goes for my career and life insights: they are what I know to be true, but not everyone has to agree with me. I will always choose honesty over saying what I think people want to hear, even when writing a book!

Everything that I've shared here with you is what I've come to learn from over fourteen years in the industry and as a business owner. From the wins and the epic fails, the laughs and the tears, to the elation and the frustration—I wanted to share it all. It's just how I operate. What you see is what you get with Roxy Jacenko!

If you take anything away from *Roxy's Little Black Book of Tips and Tricks,* I want it to be that you can find success by being you. I was the least likely pin-up girl for successful businesswomen, believe me! Nothing about my approach has ever been conventional, but I've never let that deter me. If anything, my stubbornness and determination *not* to play by the rules are precisely what's enabled me to get to where I am today. That and my unwavering work ethic. Remember, don't think Just do!

Take time to reflect on your motivation. By all means, take inspiration from what I've shared here and incorporate my tips and tricks into your career and business. But, as I've emphasised throughout the book, take ideas and make them your own. Find your motivation—what is it that drives you? What is it that you're good at and love to do, regardless of money? We all have a unique talent or idea. You've just got to run with it. And remember, you don't have to be the smartest girl or guy in the room—you've just got to be willing to go out and work for it!

To all my lovers and haters, thank you. Without you all, I wouldn't be where I am today.

Love,
Roxy xx

NOTES

NOTES

NOTES

NOTES

NOTES

NOTES